POSSIBILITY

Possibility

MICHAEL JUBIEN

CLARENDON PRESS · OXFORD

OXFORD
UNIVERSITY PRESS

Great Clarendon Street, Oxford OX2 6DP

Oxford University Press is a department of the University of Oxford.
It furthers the University's objective of excellence in research, scholarship,
and education by publishing worldwide in

Oxford New York

Auckland Cape Town Dar es Salaam Hong Kong Karachi
Kuala Lumpur Madrid Melbourne Mexico City Nairobi
New Delhi Shanghai Taipei Toronto

With offices in

Argentina Austria Brazil Chile Czech Republic France Greece
Guatemala Hungary Italy Japan Poland Portugal Singapore
South Korea Switzerland Thailand Turkey Ukraine Vietnam

Oxford is a registered trade mark of Oxford University Press
in the UK and in certain other countries

Published in the United States
by Oxford University Press Inc., New York

© Michael Jubien 2009

The moral rights of the authors have been asserted
Database right Oxford University Press (maker)

First published 2009
First published in paperback 2011

All rights reserved. No part of this publication may be reproduced,
stored in a retrieval system, or transmitted, in any form or by any means,
without the prior permission in writing of Oxford University Press,
or as expressly permitted by law, or under terms agreed with the appropriate
reprographics rights organization. Enquiries concerning reproduction
outside the scope of the above should be sent to the Rights Department,
Oxford University Press, at the address above

You must not circulate this book in any other binding or cover
and you must impose the same condition on any acquirer

British Library Cataloguing in Publication Data
Data available

Library of Congress Cataloging in Publication Data
Data available

Typeset by Laserwords Private Limited, Chennai, India
Printed in the United Kingdom by
Lightning Source UK Ltd., Milton Keynes

ISBN 978-0-19-923278-9 (Hbk)
ISBN 978-0-19-959628-7 (Pbk.)

For Judy

ACKNOWLEDGMENTS

I had the good fortune as a graduate student to have significant interaction with W. V. Quine and Saul Kripke, and as a younger faculty member with Ruth Barcan Marcus and Roderick Chisholm. These prominent philosophers have had great influence on the recent history of the central topics of this book. Their views include some of the 'orthodox' ones I will in fact be rejecting, but also views that I accept and which have influenced what is offered in these pages. I'm very grateful for these long-past interactions and for their effect on my philosophical perspective.

Scores of philosophers have my gratitude for specific comments on earlier publications and drafts and for comments at conferences, at colloquia, in conversations, and in classes, but by now there are far too many to attempt a complete list. (Most of these people have received explicit acknowledgment in previous publications, but I hope all will understand that I remain grateful if now inexplicit.) All the same, it would be wrong not to thank Chris Menzel, Karen Bennett, Linda Wetzel, Greg Ray, Kirk Ludwig, Greg Fitch, Jeff King, and David Copp. The last three have had the greatest influence on my thinking about the topics at hand and I believe this book is much better as a result.

There are eight people with whom I've spent countless hours at various times over the years discussing all manner of philosophical (and other) topics. They are Ed Gettier, Herb Heidelberger, Fred Feldman, Terry Parsons, Greg Fitch, G. J. Mattey, David Copp, and Jeff King. They have all helped shape how I think about philosophy and I'm most grateful for their friendship and for this philosophical influence. (The premature passings of Herb and, much more recently, Greg, were real losses to philosophy as well as personal losses for me and of course for many other people.)

Finally, I am very grateful to Peter Momtchiloff, for repeatedly urging me to write this book and for his help in producing it, and also to anonymous readers for Oxford University Press for their very helpful comments.

CONTENTS

Introduction   xi

1. Concrete Entities   1
    1. What is There?   1
    2. Quantifiers and Objects   2
    3. Do any Objects Persist Through Time?   9
    4. Ordinary Things and the Great Divide   15
    5. The Identities of Objects   22
    6. Mereological Essentialism   36

2. Abstract Entities   41
    1. Face Value   41
    2. Posits   43
    3. Identity Conditions   46
    4. About Properties   54

3. Against Possible Worlds   59
    1. Lewis's Analysis of Modality   59
    2. Worlds in General   67
    3. Abstract Worlds   78

4. The Core Analysis   83
    1. Speaking About Things   83
    2. Entity-Essences   88
    3. K-Essences   90

	4. Property Entailment and the Core Analysis	92
	5. Analysis and Reduction	95
	6. Essentialism and Modality *de re*	100
	7. Essentialist Thought Experiments	104
	8. Canonical Examples	107
5.	**Proper Names**	**113**
	1. Contemporary Theories	114
	2. Revisiting Intuitions and the Great Divide	128
	3. Categories and Social Determination	132
	4. Categories Redux	141
	5. A Theory of Names with Bearers	149
6.	**Fictional Names**	**159**
	1. K-essences and the 'Background' of the Story	159
	2. The Fictional Stance	163
	3. A Case Study	164
	4. Necessary Existence and Nonexistence	171
7.	**Natural Kind Terms**	**179**

References 199
Index 203

INTRODUCTION

This book aims at a unified and comprehensive presentation of views I have put forward in more or less piecemeal fashion in publications and talks over the past twenty-plus years. The metaphysical notions of possibility and necessity are the central topic. It is nearly impossible to find a recent discussion of these concepts that does not rely in one way or another on some variety of 'possible worlds'. Indeed, it is now very common to find possible-worlds talk in regions of philosophy far removed from metaphysics. But I will offer an analysis of possibility and necessity that makes no appeal to possible worlds. In fact I will urge that the possible-worlds methodology, inspired by the standard semantics of formal modal logic, actually distorts these notions rather than illuminating them or providing a plausible basis for their analysis, and this regardless of how the worlds are conceived ontologically. (I will also argue in particular that David Lewis's famous possible-worlds analysis of these notions would not be plausible even if we admitted his surprising variety of worlds into our ontology.)

The ultimate analysis of possibility and necessity, as I will suggest, does depend on two important ontological decisions. One is the choice of an analysis of the intuitive concept of a *physical object*. I offer an analysis in Chapter 1 that builds on the well-known but undeveloped account that W. V. Quine gave in *Word and Object*. Quine's project there belonged squarely to philosophical semantics, but he was very sensitive to the importance of this basic ontological concept. In contrast, I believe the recent discussion of the notion has taken place mainly in metaphysics proper while generally being ignored in philosophy of language and semantics. Most writers in these areas seem to presuppose that the notion is unproblematic. But I will argue here that central issues in philosophical semantics are very much affected by one's conception of physical objects. (For example the question of whether proper names 'refer directly' to their bearers hinges partly on how one understands this concept.) I believe further that the existing metaphysical discussion of the notion has not always been sufficiently sensitive to how we actually think and speak 'about physical objects'. Chapter 1 includes some observations about our object-talk that I think have far-reaching consequences for the topics of reference and modality. A crucial claim I defend there is that our everyday talk of objects is, simultaneously and somewhat covertly, talk of *properties*. The chapter also includes some discussion of the familiar endurance/perdurance and stuff/things debates. The ultimate account of physical objects fits naturally with the thesis of mereological essentialism, and that thesis is defended in the chapter.

The second important ontological matter is the positing of Platonic properties and relations, and that is taken up in Chapter 2. I argue that David Lewis's famous 'face value' argument in favor of *possible worlds* actually fares far better (even admirably) as a face value argument in favor of *properties*. Properties are then posited—with the unlikely inspiration of Quine—as underpinning the best overall theory, and it is argued that Quine himself would have posited properties (and other 'entia non grata') had it not been for his conviction that such entities lacked proper 'identity conditions'. The requirement of identity conditions (for any sort of entity) is then scrutinized and rejected. (I believe the pervasiveness, throughout philosophy, of the assumption that entities of various kinds need identity conditions is one unfortunate aspect of Quine's important philosophical legacy. I think it has seduced many into seeing some important philosophical problems as problems about *identity* when actually they are problems about various different concepts.) Finally, some crucial assumptions about the nature of properties are detailed.

Chapter 3 contains the considerations about possible worlds mentioned above and Chapter 4 marshals the posited properties and relations to provide the analysis of possibility and necessity, both *de dicto* and *de re*. I urge there that commonly accepted examples of *de re* necessary truths are actually false. I also argue against the widely accepted characterization of the doctrine of 'essentialism' as the acceptance of nontrivial *de re* necessity. Here I lean on the discussion in Chapter 1 of how we actually think and speak of objects, and this leads to what I believe is a more satisfactory account of the doctrine of essentialism.

The discussions of Chapters 1–4 proceed as far as possible without relying on any particular theory of proper names. The business of Chapter 5 is to offer a theory of names with bearers, and names without bearers are taken up in Chapter 6. I argue that names with bearers do not 'refer directly' to those bearers, but instead express certain distinctive properties that their bearers possess, and that these properties, rather than the bearers themselves, are the rightful 'constituents' of the intuitive propositions expressed by sentences containing the names. I claim that the properties that names express are fixed by how the names are used by speakers in general—what I call social determination—and notably not by anything that is said or thought by a person introducing a name. An important consequence of this treatment is that the usual view—inspired by first-order logic—of the 'logical form' of subject/predicate sentences whose subjects are names is incorrect (and that this has a further consequence for what are commonly regarded as 'identity sentences'). In Chapter 6 I argue that 'empty' names behave in close analogy with the behavior of names that have bearers. There I also address the important (and independently interesting) topic of necessary existence and nonexistence, which has much to do with the conception of 'fictional entities' offered in the chapter.

The topic of 'natural kind' terms is taken up in Chapter 7. The contemporary view of such terms was strongly influenced by Saul Kripke's discussion 'in *Naming and Necessity* and by Hilary Putnam's discussion in 'The Meaning of "Meaning"'. Kripke argued that 'natural kind' terms like 'water', 'gold', and 'tiger' function very much as proper names do, and this conviction led directly to his conclusions about these terms. I agree with the general claim of functional parallelism, but since I adopt a different conception of names, my treatment of the natural kind terms is also different. I argue that the meanings of these terms are socially determined in much the way the properties that names express are socially determined. Then I argue from this standpoint that the familiar and influential examples of supposed necessary a posteriori truths advanced by Kripke and by Putnam do not succeed.

Thus I am defending an overall cluster of views that is very much at odds with the current 'orthodoxy'. Each of these views, taken in isolation from the rest, may seem implausible from the orthodox standpoint, which of course has an impressive internal coherence. But I think the package of views I am offering is no less coherent and, on the whole, fits better with how we actually think and speak about the world. Thus I hope readers will have the forbearance to see the entire package unfold before dismissing any of its parts.

In developing and presenting these views here and there over the years, and just in staying alert to the flow of the profession, I have continually been impressed by how deeply entrenched and widespread the orthodox doctrines really are. This of course is partly the result of the power of the ideas themselves (and perhaps also the persuasiveness and charisma of their main proponents). But I think another factor is that formal logic, both modal and nonmodal, has evolved and been applied in ways that happen to tilt in favor of the orthodox positions, but without having been crafted with such a goal in view. (As a simple example, first-order logic tilts in favor of the 'direct reference' account of proper names by using individual constants to play the intuitive role of names, and by 'interpreting' the constants simply as the individuals that are assigned to them for the purpose of generating truth values.) This tilting may encourage a feeling that the orthodox views have the *imprimatur* of logic itself, and that to oppose them is somehow to flout logic. I oppose the orthodoxy but have always had great respect for logic. Thus an undercurrent in this book will surface at a number of points, where I insist that it is easy to be misled by logic, that logic, pure and unassailable in itself, does not provide philosophical silver bullets, and that it has in fact been misapplied at certain important moments in the history of our topics with unhappy results. It will emerge in these pages that I believe it has often been uncritically assumed of what was in fact initially a tool for clarifying mathematics, that it could be applied seamlessly and uniformly in the effort to clarify ordinary language and philosophy, and that this has been a real mistake.

I

CONCRETE ENTITIES

1. What is There?

TAKING this question as one about the contents of the physical world, I think the most general and 'naturalistic' answer is that there is a great deal of physical matter strewn about in spacetime.[1] This answer takes no stand on whether 'matter' somehow includes packets or fields of energy, on whether matter is composed of 'particles', nor on whether matter is ultimately just 'crimped' spacetime. The answer also says nothing about whether matter persists through time, and it has the further virtue of saying nothing at all about *objects*. It's a very preliminary and noncommittal answer, but it isn't trivial. It exploits our intuitive concept of *matter* without invoking the dicey concept of *object*.

So it is hard to see how anyone but an idealist could object to it. Surely there is lots of matter in spacetime, regardless of how we might come to analyze either matter or spacetime. In everyday life we view some of that matter as the sun, some as the moon, some as tables and chairs, some as dogs and cats, and so forth. But then we make a leap: we generalize and think of them all as individual *things* or *objects*. As W. V. Quine put

---

[1] Here I mean to include whatever 'dark' (including 'nonbaryonic') matter there may be.

it, '[w]e are prone to talk and think of objects'.[2] But as soon as we do, trouble sets in. Are the objects already there, or are they somehow our own conceptual imposition on what's already there? This question has troubled many philosophers and has led to some genuinely exotic positions, but I believe it has a fairly simple answer and I'll try to provide it in the next section.

Quine offered the following very general and liberal characterization of objects: a *physical object* '... comprises simply the content, however heterogeneous, of some portion of spacetime, however disconnected and gerrymandered'.[3] I will call this characterization 'Q'. Q goes at least part of the way toward answering our recent question about objects, for certainly the content, that is the 'matter', of a region of spacetime is indeed 'already there'. We will soon see that I think Q is best understood in a way that actually goes the full distance toward an answer. But for the moment notice only that it meshes nicely with our answer to the original question and evidently does so in a naturalistic way.

2. Quantifiers and Objects

Some people may agree wholeheartedly that there is lots of matter spread around in spacetime but nevertheless reject Q. The reason is that Q admits all manner of grossly scattered objects, instantaneous objects, and objects lacking spatial extension, but we do not normally think of most of these 'Q-objects' as *objects*. This everyday inclination has its philosophical defenders. For example there are those who—thinking of grossly scattered objects—ask, 'When does composition occur?', and seek an answer in the form of necessary and sufficient conditions that rule out most exotic Q-objects and rule in (some or all) everyday objects. Others hold that 'composition

[2] Quine (1969: 1).   [3] Quine (1960: 171).

always occurs' and even claim it is an objective fact about the world that all of these objects exist.[4] Indeed, that view seems entirely compatible with Q.

Despite this, I think it threatens to be a quasi-mystical way of viewing the matter. It's as if there's a very special, insensible phenomenon known as 'composition', which in some cases unites spatiotemporally separated objects into a single object but perhaps in other cases does not. Even one who thinks 'composition always occurs' has signed on for this potentially unfortunate way of conceiving the matter. I think there is a much better way, and I will detail it soon. But for the moment let's look at a concrete example.

Suppose you are looking at two-piece suits on the rack at your favorite haberdashery. You focus on a certain suit and notice that right next to it is another in exactly the same pattern, color, and size, from the same maker, etc. In the interest of simplicity, imagine that they are qualitatively indistinguishable. Now suppose further that you agree that two-piece suits are physical objects, so that you have no blanket objection to grossly scattered objects, but that you are an ordinary person and so recognize far fewer of them than does Q. Should you then deny that there is a physical object composed of the trousers of one of the suits and the jacket of the other? Should you say that (pairwise) 'composition has occurred' only twice here? Like anyone else, you will certainly want to say that there are only two *suits* here, not four. But it doesn't follow that there are only two (grossly scattered) *objects*. Not all suit-like objects need be suits.

Notice that since we've assumed qualitative indistinguishability, the two two-piece combinations that aren't suits do not differ intrinsically from the two that are. This suggests, very strongly I think, that what makes a given combination a *suit* is some relation it bears to something else, in this case perhaps

---

[4] See Sider (2001) for a defense of this position. A representative philosopher who denies 'universal composition' is van Inwagen (1987, 1990b, 1994).

something as simple as (having certain structural features and) being offered for sale as a suit.[5] It may also suggest that if any of these scattered combinations is a physical object, then they all are. But I think that if it does suggest this, that is because we are thinking that *being an object* is intrinsic to objects, and I don't think this can be right. I think *being an object* (like *being a suit*) is a relational property—an intentional one at that—and I'll now try to develop this thought.

Let's begin by considering the following three ordinary sentences:

(1) Some crows like shiny objects.
(2) Some crows ate the pie.
(3) Some wine stained the carpet.

In our early days in logic class we were taught to 'translate' (1) into the language of logic as if it meant that at least one crow likes shiny objects. Of course in idiomatic English it probably does not quite mean this, but rather means something that entails that more than one crow likes shiny objects. Either way, we are inclined to think of 'some' in (1) as functioning as a *singular objectual quantifier*. It is 'objectual' because it ranges over *objects* and 'singular' because it is interpreted as doing so individually, that is, one at a time. This cannot be said for the role 'some' plays in sentence (2), which does not mean that at least one crow ate the pie. Nor does it mean that each of a few (or several) crows ate the pie. We cannot adequately capture (2) with the singular objectual quantifier. (2), on its most natural

---

[5] It is also worth noticing the awkwardness of denying that such a combination is an object, for one cannot consistently use terms like 'combination'. One must instead scrupulously avoid substantive nouns and noun phrases that invite quantification, saying instead that a certain pair of pants and jacket do not constitute an object. One cannot reasonably say that the (mereological) sum of those items exists but is not an object. One must deny that there is a sum of those items in the first place. But then we have the apparent consequence that whether a sum exists depends on whether the stuff in question has a certain sort of relational property, and often (as in this case) one that is intentional in nature.

reading, says that some crows *collectively* ate the pie, that is, that some crows are such that each of them ate some of the pie and that they did so in such a way that none of the pie remained. So (2) speaks *plurally* of objects and requires that 'some' be understood as a 'plural' (objectual) quantifier.[6]

In (3) we have another appearance of 'some' and yet another type of quantifier. We may call it a *stuff* or *mass quantifier*. Thus, and very roughly, when 'some' is followed by a mass noun like 'wine', it should be understood as a mass quantifier and when followed by a count noun like 'crow' (or 'crows'), as an objectual quantifier. (Of course sometimes 'wine' is a count noun, as in 'Kent bid on some wines at the auction'; and 'crow' is at least available as a mass term, though it is often so used in an unappetizing metaphorical way.) There is no reasonable way to capture the meaning of (3) with the resources of (singular or plural) objectual quantification—*given our ordinary understanding of what counts as an object*. Under that understanding, a scattered quantity of liquid simply doesn't count as an object.

Mass quantification is a phenomenon unto itself, embedded deeply and irreducibly in our language *as we normally use it*. A couple of its features are worth noticing. One is that the correct use of a mass quantifier carries no presupposition that the 'mass' in question is not composed of individual objects or even of a single object. The claim that some stuff in the closet needs to be laundered will be true even though the stuff in question consists solely of articles of clothing. And the claim that some stuff has clogged the drain remains true even when it is later discovered that the stuff in question is a golf ball. Mass quantification is therefore extremely flexible as a result of our having mass terms like 'stuff' (and 'matter', 'junk', 'dreck', etc.) that apply correctly to discrete pluralities of unquestionable everyday objects, and even to individual such objects.

---

[6] George Boolos was an early and effective champion of plural quantification. See, e.g., Boolos (1984).

A second important fact about mass quantification is that it enables us to quantify without qualm over all Q-objects, for we may easily speak of 'the matter (or stuff) of region R', where R is any spacetime region whatsoever. Surely we already quantify objectually over arbitrary regions of spacetime. Indeed Quine did so in advancing Q and no one would have thought to complain that he was somehow abusing the language or not speaking literally. Combining this with the promiscuous generality of mass terms like 'stuff' and 'matter' (and Quine's 'content', etc.) yields the conclusion that sentences of our language contain mass quantifiers that *already* range over every Q-object, and that there is nothing metaphysically suspect or revolutionary about this at all. Nor does any of this depend on assuming that maximal 'composition' has occurred (whatever that might mean) or anything of the kind. It's just a fact that there is matter in spacetime and that we may and do routinely quantify over *any of it*.

So what could it mean to say that the range of this promiscuous mass quantification includes both objects and non-objects? I think there are three basic possibilities. One is the idea that objects have that status because of how they are in themselves and that this is just a primitive fact about the world. The second is that a 'phenomenon' like composition or *objectification* (for a more general term that would cover *de*composition as well) has occurred in some of these cases but not in others. The third is to take the claim just as a report about how we use our everyday objectual quantifiers.

Notice that the only fuel for skepticism about Q is indeed the way we use quantifiers in everyday life. But we have seen a clear example in which we allow quantification in one case and disallow it in another, where the cases in question are intrinsically indistinguishable. It would not be difficult to produce further examples. So someone who favors the first possibility faces a severe mismatch between ordinary quantification and the world's objects.

Quantifiers and Objects

The second possibility—'objectification'—comes in two versions, one naturalistic, the other not. The naturalistic version is really just a variation on the third major possibility: that objectification happens as a result of our treating some matter as an object, that we confer objecthood upon any matter simply by thinking and speaking of that matter as an object, that is, by quantifying over it objectually (and invoking count nouns, etc., for it). This is analogous to the case of the suit. Some matter gets to be a *suit*, roughly, if part of it is an appropriate pair of pants, the rest of it is an appropriate jacket, *and we treat their mereological sum in certain characteristic ways*. In both cases, some matter comes to enjoy a certain status—*object* or *suit*—partly but crucially as a result of having a certain intentional (and relational) property.

The non-naturalistic version of the second possibility is the above mentioned, quasi-mystical idea that a rarefied phenomenon in the world often anoints some matter as an object but often refrains from so anointing other matter, sometimes even intrinsically indistinguishable matter, and that this phenomenon just happens to match how we normally use the word 'object' and how we quantify objectually over the world's contents. It is clear that one should adopt this view only as a last resort and in fact we won't have to consider it again.

Now, it is certainly correct that we don't normally apply the terms 'object' and 'thing' (etc.) to arbitrary Q-objects, and that we don't include the majority of them in the range of our everyday objectual quantifiers. But precisely because the first possibility (primitive objecthood) and the quasi-mystical version of the second (rarefied objectification) have been rejected, there is no principled reason why we cannot or should not. (Indeed, it is clear that we already have significant variation in the idiolects of competent speakers as to what is counted as an object. It really is up to—and therefore relative to—us.)

This is how I believe Q should be understood. It is a *conventional* decision—adopted for use in metaphysics and semantics—to use objectual quantifiers so that their range *exactly matches* the already established range of our mass quantifiers. Crudely put, because there is no intrinsic difference between the chosen suit and either 'non-suit', this decision is utterly benign metaphysically. It does not inflate the physical universe beyond what is actually there. Nor does it flout our most general naturalistic concept of a physical object—objects are still just things composed of matter like they always were. It is merely a conventional decision about how to use a certain sort of quantifier, in this case a convention made in the interest of smooth systematic metaphysics and semantics. When we see Q in this way as a technical convention about quantifier management, we are in a position to answer the question about whether the world's objects were 'already there', or whether they are a 'conceptual imposition' upon what's already there.

The answer is: *both*! The reason is that the very question makes sense only with respect to a prior understanding of 'object', and that since any such understanding is a matter of convention, whether some matter counts or doesn't count as an object is a conceptual imposition on the physical world. But because *under* any such convention, any *object* is simply some matter over which the participants in the convention are quantifying objectually, the objects, under that convention, were of course already there. Under any given such convention, the difference between 'the matter in spacetime region R' and 'the object in spacetime region R' is merely a difference in grammar, not a difference in ontological status. We could, in principle, give a complete account of physics and the physical world without ever using an objectual quantifier. And we could do the same using objectual quantifiers under any convention at all, from very minimalist choices all the way to the maximal Q.[7] Surely, since we are indeed 'prone to talk and think of

---

[7] Of course Q is maximal only given that we are not entertaining the idea that there can be more than one object fully occupying a given spacetime region.

objects', it is easier to indulge in this tendency with the help of objectual quantifiers, and probably easiest with ones that range maximally (at least once we get used to it). It is also liberating, when we turn to the metaphysics of everyday objects, to have the capability of describing matters from this maximal and uniform perspective.

To be an object (or 'thing'), with respect to a given convention, is then simply to be thought of and spoken of, under that convention, in a certain *grammatical* way, a way that features objectual quantification and reference by means of count nouns. It is thus an intentional (and relational) property of the things that have it; it is neither an intrinsic property nor a relational property involving other parts of the non-intentional world. Nothing has such a property absolutely, but only relative to a given convention. Any such convention settles *what objects there are*, but only as a function of *what there is*. *What there is* stands as an objective, mind-independent feature of reality. *What objects there are* is the outcome of a convention for speaking about this given reality. Different conventions differ as to how many objects there are, but they do not differ as to what there is. Convention Q will prevail in the remainder of this book. Thus, any physical matter is an *object*, an object that was 'already there', but which we need not have spoken of in such objectual terms.

3. Do any Objects Persist Through Time?

The recent metaphysical literature contains much discussion of 'endurantism' and 'perdurantism'.[8] These are rival views about whether objects, especially ordinary ones like tables and chairs,

---

[8] A few more recent among the many writers on this topic are Baker (1997, 2000), Heller (1990), Jubien (1993), Lewis (1986), Merricks (1995, 1999), Sider (2001), and van Inwagen (1990a, 1990b).

are three-dimensional entities that may be 'entirely present' at different moments, or whether they are four-dimensional entities of which only different three-dimensional parts may be present at different moments. These views may be seen as different ways of coping with a philosophical puzzle about 'change': how best to reconcile our everyday belief that 'objects' persist through time with our everyday conviction that these same 'objects' may have incompatible properties at different times.

Very roughly, the endurantist position takes the first belief at face value, holding that one and the same object is indeed 'entirely present' at different times. The barn that we saw on Monday is the very same object that we now see on Friday: it has *endured* through time. But now an endurantist has to explain how it could be that a single object that, say, had no cupola on Monday can have one today. The Principle of the Indiscernibility of Identicals holds that if x and y are (numerically) identical, then x and y have exactly the same properties. This principle is seemingly indisputable and is accepted by all (or nearly all) parties in the present discussion. But it evidently entails that if the relation of (numerical) identity really holds between the object that was present on Monday and the one that is present today, then it is a barn without a cupola that is present today. Endurantists have different strategies for dealing with this puzzle.

In contrast, the perdurantist view is that the barn does not literally persist through time. Ordinary objects like barns are held not to be three-dimensional things that endure. Instead they are four-dimensional 'spacetime worms', and the earlier and later parts of these worms are entirely distinct—they don't overlap at all. So the perdurantist gives a nonliteral reinterpretation of the everyday belief in persistence: things persist through time by being temporally extended entities that have different parts at different times. They persist by *perduring*, not by enduring. Perdurantists thus have an easy

Do any Objects Persist Through Time?

answer to the puzzle. The Indiscernibility of Identicals is irrelevant because the object that was here on Monday is *not* (identical with) the one that is here today. So there's no pressure to think they should both lack cupolas (or both have cupolas). The barn simply has different 'temporal parts' that themselves may have different intuitive parts and different properties generally.

It is clear that in everyday life we think of ordinary items like barns as if they were three-dimensional objects that are wholly present on different occasions—we are, so to speak, naïve endurantists about such objects. So a coherent endurantist account would at first seem to have the advantage of squaring nicely with how we normally think and speak. But, as we just saw, such an account has to deal convincingly with the intuitive belief that such objects gain and lose parts over time, and change in other ways as well, and it has been surprisingly difficult for proponents of the view to reach consensus on a specific account. Without discussing the matter in detail, we may mention two among a number of options that have been considered. One is the idea that all properties are relativized to times, so that the barn both *has-no-cupola*$_{Monday}$ and *has-a-cupola*$_{Friday}$. A given intuitive property is thus displaced by infinitely many properties differing only in their temporal 'indices'. In general the time-relativized analogue of any intuitive property is compatible with its negation relativized to a different time. A second approach, similar in spirit but ontologically different, is to hold that the instantiation itself is a ternary rather than a binary relation. Under this approach, it is literally ungrammatical to say that the barn has or does not have a cupola without also specifying a time. In general, for an object to instantiate a property at one time is compatible with its failing to instantiate it at another (and with its instantiating its negation at another time).

On the other hand, and as we have glimpsed, a coherent perdurantist account doesn't seem to require any modification in the way we ordinarily think of properties or instantiation.[9] There is an ontological difference, but at the concrete rather than the abstract level. The only apparent drawback for perdurantism is the required (and rather extensive) reinterpretation of things we normally say and think as a result of our everyday naïve endurantism.[10] But the reinterpretation is simple and systematic, and it may reasonably be viewed more as an inconvenience than as a substantive shortcoming.

It has also been held that the two strategies are essentially 'notational variants' of each other so that there is nothing much at stake philosophically in the ongoing discussion.[11] I have some sympathy with this appraisal, but I don't think it is entirely correct. Again sparing details, the reason is that I believe any three-dimensional strategy ultimately requires significant adjustments in our ordinary way of thinking about properties and instantiation in order to reconcile 'change over time' with the Indiscernibility of Identicals, and there are substantively different such adjustments available as we saw. But no comparable adjustments seemed needed for a coherent perdurantist account. So I suspect it cannot be entirely right that there is nothing at stake in the discussion. For example it seems to me that there is already something at stake between the two endurantist strategies we mentioned.

Despite this, there is some appeal in the idea that there is nothing about the *concrete* world that ensures that one of these accounts is right, the other wrong. There is a strong initial whiff of conventionality in the atmosphere of the discussion. What is its source?

---

[9] Not that there are no differences among perdurantist accounts. For example Sider (2001) offers a theory that differs in a central way from what may be thought of as the standard view.

[10] As an example, when we say 'The barn we saw on Friday had a cupola', this must be understood as meaning that the Friday-part of a cupola was part of the Friday-part of the barn that our Friday-parts saw.

[11] For example this is Eli Hirsch's position. See Hirsch (1982).

Do any Objects Persist Through Time?

Our initial question in this section was 'Do any objects persist through time?' This may be thought to raise another question: 'Is there a fact of the matter?' If the idea that there is 'no fact of the matter' were defensible, it would be natural to think we should choose between three- and four-dimensional treatments on grounds of convenience or esthetics, etc. In short, it would seem that we simply need a convention. I'm going to suggest that there is a fact of the matter, but one that we're epistemically incapable of discerning, and that for this reason we're forced into the realm of convention.

Consider a tiny bit of matter, say a 'proton' or, better, a *point-sized* bit p, located at some spatial position at time t.[12] Suppose that a qualitatively indistinguishable object p* is located at some position at the later time t*, and that there is a continuous path in spacetime connecting p and p*, each instantaneous 'slice' of which contains a qualitatively indistinguishable object. How could we possibly determine whether p is identical with p* (and with each of the objects on the path)? There is no conceivable test that would settle this question. Neither identity nor, of course, diversity follows from qualitative indiscernibility. Yet it does seem to be a genuine question concerning a real fact of the matter.

We are able to conceive of time as if it were like a river 'flowing past' p over the interval, so that p is present throughout and p = p*. But we are also able to conceive of p as if it were part of an 'instantaneous frame' in a movie composed of continuum-many frames, all distinct but ordered in a certain way, so that p is a different object from p* and from all the other p-like objects that appear and disappear continuously over the interval.[13] But we evidently have no way of knowing whether the universe is unfolding in the manner of the river or

---

[12] Note that if x is a (dimensionless) *point* in any spacetime region that is fully occupied by matter, then Q entails that there is an object exactly occupying x.

[13] The 'river' and 'movie' conceptions correspond respectively (and roughly) to McTaggart's famous 'A-series' and 'B-series'. See McTaggart (1927), chapter 33.

the movie. At the very least there is no conceivable empirical test that would settle the matter. Given this, and assuming that both perdurantism and endurantism are coherent, it seems a priori impossible that there could be a convincing philosophical argument establishing either over its rival.[14]

So I think there is an epistemic hurdle we are in principle unable to clear, and that what is needed is a convention. The convention I prefer is the 'movie' conception on which we proceed *as if* p were distinct from p* (and from every other object on the path), regardless of whether that is the actual fact of the matter. We will never know, but there is an important way in which it shouldn't matter, because any conclusions reached under this convention should map readily onto conclusions driven by the other (and vice versa). (This is the grain of truth in the 'notational variant' or 'verbal dispute' position. What is a bit misleading about that position is that there may be substantively different ways of elaborating either convention.)

I will thus proceed as if perdurance is the way of the world, so that ordinary objects like barns are treated as if they were four-dimensional spacetime 'worms' all of whose parts have a temporal aspect. I have already noted that this is a considerable departure from everyday naïve endurantism. That might seem a disadvantage, but I believe it is at worst very minor because it is routine (though sometimes tedious) to translate everyday thoughts into the perdurantist vocabulary. Moreover, we are doing metaphysics, not embarking on a mission to transform everyday thinking, so we should be able to handle it.

Finally, there is a major advantage to the perdurance convention. For the everyday thought that medium-sized objects

---

[14] This has not prevented some from trying. One notable effort is to be found in Sider (2001). I believe Sider's argument ultimately rests on the mistake of presuming that *being an object* is intrinsic to the things that instantiate it instead of an intentional relational property reflecting a quantifier convention, as argued above.

endure in the way that p endures under the 'river' convention is simply incorrect. Even if the tiny bits of matter of which everyday objects are composed endure, it is not true that these ordinary objects do, for they are gaining and losing such parts continually. So everyday thinking really appears to offer no decisive reason for preferring the river convention after all.

4. Ordinary Things and the Great Divide

We are so far assuming that ordinary things—objects of familiar kinds—are to be found among the objects acknowledged by Q and also that they are four-dimensional spacetime worms. For the moment, however, I want to set the latter position aside and consider certain further aspects of our everyday thinking about ordinary things.

There is a 'great divide' apparent in such thinking. On the one hand, we are able to think about ordinary things merely as physical objects. On the other hand, we also think of them as objects of familiar kinds. One and the same object, for example, may be thought of purely as a physical object, or as a piece of clay, or as a statue. Another may be thought of as a planet, as a celestial body, or again merely as a physical object, and so on. Any ordinary object may be thought of just as an object, or thought of as an object of any number of different familiar kinds. So far this is unsurprising. But it has a remarkable further feature: the different ways of thinking about a given thing are accompanied by differing attitudes about its *parts* and about the *arrangement* of its parts. As a very general observation, when thought of just as an object, the parts of a thing seem definitive and their arrangement seems inconsequential. But when thought of as an object of a familiar kind there is a striking reversal: we think of the arrangement as important and the parts themselves as inessential. This division in our thinking at first may seem to threaten inconsistency or incoherence. Let's explore the matter further.

A good illustration of the divide is provided by the familiar *Ship of Theseus* story. Consider the version in which (suppressing perdurance) the 'original parts' are collected and reassembled in the original way. Thinking about the original ship as a *ship*, in our everyday way, we don't hesitate to think that we continue to have 'the same ship' as each part is replaced. (Notice also that licensing agencies and ship registries, yacht clubs, law enforcement authorities, insurance companies and the like perform their various roles under the same conviction.) Assuming that we continue to think this even when all of the 'original parts' have been replaced by like parts, it is already out of the question that the other ship is the original ship. After all, there are two ships afloat now, not one. Both cannot be the single ship we started with.

So why does anyone feel puzzlement? It depends partly on the further fact that when we think of the original ship and the outcome of the reassembly merely as *physical objects*, and not specifically as *ships*, it is very compelling to think they are one and the same physical object. But we will soon see that the real reason for the puzzlement lies well beneath the surface of these facts about everyday thought.

To generalize a little, what is going on here is that when we think of something as a *ship*, its actual parts have little or no significance to us. This is borne out in our (and the agencies', etc.) readiness to think the ship survives each successive replacement. On the other hand, the arrangement of the parts is very important to us. If we were to wind up rearranging the parts as we replaced them, so that what was once a sloop was gradually transformed into a bungalow, or even a catamaran, we would certainly think we no longer had the original vessel.

But notice, more generally, what happens when we think of something merely as a physical object. Take first a piece of clay, but consider it only as a physical object, not as a piece of clay (for *piece of clay* is a familiar kind). We can distort this object any way we choose and still have one and the same object. Under Q we could even scatter it as widely as we like, and we would still have the same object though, of course, it would no longer be a piece of clay. It's the parts that settle this for us, and their arrangement is irrelevant. This is why, returning to the *Ship of Theseus*, we tend to think the reassembled original parts comprise the original physical object. That they were reassembled in the original way elevates the sense of mystery, because arrangement matters for ships, but the intuition that we have the same object is really driven only by the identities of the parts. If they had been arranged differently we would have the same intuition—it would have counted as the same object whether it remained a ship or not.

Thus, and to emphasize, when we think of something merely as a physical object, its parts are definitive and their arrangement is irrelevant. Roughly the reverse happens, though to varying degrees, when we think of something as an object of a familiar kind. The parts are more or less irrelevant but their arrangement is more or less essential. This side of the divide tolerates real variation depending on just what familiar kind is in play. For example suppose we have a clay statue. Intuitively, it's a physical object that also falls under two prominent familiar kinds: *piece of clay* and *statue*. But the arrangement of its parts is more important when we think of it as a statue than when we think of it as a piece of clay. A typical clay statue can survive only so much distortion and retain its status as the statue, but the very same object can survive arbitrary (intact) distortion while remaining the piece of clay.[15]

---

[15] Similarly, there are entities of some familiar kinds that would not survive replacement of certain of their parts in certain ways, even by qualitatively indiscernible objects. Museums and tombs, for example, have that status partly because of the entities they are designed to honor and preserve. There are 'Dali museums' in Barcelona and Tampa. Although probably no specific works are essential to either museum's having that status, it is certainly true that if all the

I believe all of these remarks are simply empirical generalizations about how we in fact think and speak of objects. To repeat, when we think of them just as physical objects, their parts are paramount but their arrangement doesn't matter. But when we think of them as objects of familiar kinds, the parts recede in importance and their arrangement becomes critical. This is the great divide, and I believe we should take it very seriously in pursuing metaphysics and philosophy of language. One of the main goals of this book is to arrive at a proper understanding and accommodation of the divide. I will now try to suggest why this is a worthy goal.

It might be thought that it isn't. Thus someone might say: 'I concede that there is such a divide in our everyday thinking, but I also think it's nothing but trouble and should be avoided, not accommodated, in our philosophical thinking. The *Ship of Theseus* gives perfect evidence. It is obviously inconsistent to think that the entity resulting from the replacements is the *Ship of Theseus* while also holding that the entity resulting from reassembly is the very one we started with. A ship is just a physical object. Same object, same ship. Something has to give, and it should be one side of the divide or the other. There are no alternatives.'

I believe this reasoning rests on a hidden presupposition, one that really should be rejected, and that the appearance of inconsistency vanishes when we do reject it. The presupposition is deep seated and unfortunately is reinforced by our typical philosophers' way of translating ordinary sentences into the language of logic. One way to state it is as follows. We

---

works of either were replaced by qualitatively indistinguishable fakes, it would no longer really be a Dali museum. On the other hand, such a museum could survive a total replacement of its parts, provided that the actual works were replaced by genuine works of the artist. For example, Barcelona and Tampa could agree to swap their entire collections. (Tampa would be the loser here.) It is also true that there is great latitude in how the parts of a specific *museum* may be arranged, perhaps even more in the case of Dali than in the case of a typical museum. I will not pursue details.

tend to think that because it is a single object that falls under various kinds (including the kind *object*), whatever we truly say 'of that object' when thinking about it as an object of one kind must also hold 'of it' when we think of it as an object of any of its other kinds. To illustrate, if a sentence 'That statue has property P' is true, then we automatically tend to think that 'That piece of clay has property P' must also be true, and similarly for 'That object has property P'. We think this because it is just one object that is both the statue and the piece of clay (and, of course, the object). Roughly speaking, we tend to think sentences like these are just 'about' a certain *object* and not 'about' anything else. We act as if the different demonstrative phrases serve merely to pick out the object we aim to say something about, and then play no further role in what will be said.

But here is a little evidence that this tendency of thought isn't really right, at least not in full generality. Suppose a sculptor fashions a statue from a particularly stiff and unyielding piece of clay. At the end he might easily say, 'I love the statue but I really hate that piece of clay—it's way too hard to work'. This would be a perfectly natural and reasonable thing to say and it cannot seriously be doubted that under the right sorts of circumstances it would be true. But of course there is only one object under discussion and (fancy psychology aside) it cannot be that the sculptor at once both loves and hates *it*. (He is fully aware that 'the statue *is* the piece of clay', so his epistemic situation is unlike Lois Lane's with respect to Superman and Clark Kent.) What this suggests to me is that the statement is *not* just about a certain object. Speaking intuitively, it is partly about that object *qua* statue and partly about that same object *qua* piece of clay. The kinds *statue* and *piece of clay* are *somehow* implicated in the content of the sentence, and do not serve merely to pick out an object.

Here is another example I have used in the past. Suppose someone is given an olive-sized object and reacts by saying

'Omigod it's so *big*!' The object in question is a diamond, set in a gold ring. Is the reaction merely about that *object*? I don't see how it could be. We would not normally think the person had been given a big physical object. We would normally think the object was big *for a diamond* but not big *for a physical object*. It simply doesn't follow that it's a big object even though the diamond is of course the object. That single object is big *qua* diamond but *not* big *qua* object. So, intuitively, the exuberant reaction is implicitly about the object *qua* diamond. It isn't *just* about the object. It is somehow about the *kind* as well.

For a final example let's recall the famous puzzle about the statue and the piece of clay (around which we have so far tiptoed). We think that the piece of clay could survive extensive reshaping but the statue could not. What makes this seem puzzling? It's this. We tend to think that when we utter 'The piece of clay could survive extensive reshaping', we are merely saying something about an object that we happened to pick out with the phrase 'the piece of clay'; and when we utter 'The statue could not …', we think we're merely speaking about an object that we happened to pick out with the phrase 'the statue'. But if these thoughts were correct, then there would have to be two objects under discussion, not one. This is now very puzzling because at the outset we also thought that the two phrases picked out one and the same object by exploiting different descriptions it happened to satisfy. I want to suggest that the puzzle evaporates when we stop thinking that the statements are only about certain *objects*. They are also about (different) *kinds* (of objects). In Chapter 4 I will say just how I think the kinds come into play in the intuitive propositions expressed by sentences like the ones we've been considering.

The tendency to think that in statements like these we pick out an object and then make assertions that are solely about *it* will be called *object fixation*. In effect, we are fixating on the *object* and ignoring the *kind* once it has performed its individuative chore. (So we might also call the tendency *kind repression*.)

Here is how object fixation drives the above mentioned suspicion about the great divide based on the *Ship of Theseus* case. Let's quickly review the facts. First, the familiar-kind/arrangement side of the divide encourages us to think the result of the replacements is the (original) ship, the *Ship of Theseus*. Next, the object/parts side of the divide encourages us to think that the result of the reassembly is the original *object*. Then the critic says we can't have it both ways because 'the object *is* the ship'. This is object fixation because it is taken to license inferences from statements 'about the object' to conclusions 'about the ship', and vice versa. ('After all, it's just one thing!') But if we avoid this fixation, we can indeed have it both ways and also dispel the puzzle. To avoid object fixation is to recognize that various statements are not just about objects, but rather are somehow about objects *qua* different *kinds*. One of the kinds here is (*specific*) *object*; the other is (*specific*) *ship*.

At the beginning of the story we have a certain object that falls under the kind of being a certain *specific* ship (the *Ship of Theseus*). As the story unfolds we have a succession of (somewhat) different objects continuing to be of this same kind, for each of them, in its turn, is of the kind *Ship of Theseus*. At the end we have an entirely different object that is nevertheless still of this kind. And we also have another object of the (general) kind *ship*, but of course not of the kind *Ship of Theseus*. This object happens to be the original object or, to give it a parallel statement, it happens to be of the kind *such and such* (*original*) *object*.

For this to be puzzling one must think either that it would follow from the fact that something is the original object that it is also the *Ship of Theseus*, or else that it would follow from the fact that something is the *Ship of Theseus* that it is also the original object. But these would be object-fixated inferences, taking us from a statement about something *qua* object to a statement about something *qua* ship, or vice versa. We may reject these inferences and maintain both the object/parts-driven intuition that a given object was once the ship but is no longer, and also the familiar-kind/arrangement-driven intuition that a completely different object from the original is now the ship. The puzzlement disappears with the object fixation.

In what follows I will develop more detail about object fixation, about its unfortunate enshrinement in philosophers' routine deployment of logic, and about how to avoid it. We have already seen a rough indication of how a couple of familiar metaphysical puzzles depend on the fixation. As this book unfolds we will come to see how certain important and influential philosophical positions also depend on it, and how the rejection of these object-fixated positions enables us to gain a clearer view of modality and names. One such position will be up for discussion in Section 6.[16]

5. The Identities of Objects

Every object is of course a particular object. But in what does the *particularity* (or *specificity* or *identity*) of a given object consist? What makes an object the specific object that it is? In adopting convention Q along with perdurance (hereafter 'QP') we accomplished two things. With Q we decided how we would quantify objectually over the given contents of the world. Then, with perdurance, we decided that objects would

---

[16] Some time after arriving at the notions of the great divide and object fixation, I learned from Pavel Materna that Pavel Tichý had pursued similar lines of thought in the past, but with different terminology and detail. These ideas played a role in the development of his 'transparent intensional logic'. See, e.g., Tichý (1987). A key difference between his ultimate approach and mine is his reliance on possible worlds.

The Identities of Objects

be viewed as confined to the times at which they exist—that they would not be viewed as 'enduring' through time. But this double convention does not yet fully delineate our concept of *object* because it leaves open questions about what *might* have been true for the objects we recognize. For example, we may ask whether a given object might have been located somewhere else.

The answer to this question has to depend on whether and to what extent we conceive an object's location to contribute to its being the object that it is. Nothing about QP, together with the actual features and configuration of the world's matter, can settle this question. Our position is somewhat analogous to the earlier dilemma (in Section 3) of whether the 'point-objects' p and p* are identical. We found ourselves able to conceive of p and p* either as one object or as two. We chose the latter in adopting the perdurance convention. But now, just as there was no conceivable empirical test that could settle the question of the identity of p and p*, there is no conceivable empirical test that could settle the question of whether a given object might have been somewhere else (at a given time). When Quine said we are prone to talk and think of objects, he might have added that we are prone to doing so in a comprehensive way, one that takes questions like the present modal one to be meaningful and to require answers. So we need a third convention to add to the dyadic QP. The first convention determines what matter constitutes objects. The second determines whether there are different temporal possibilities for a given object. Now the third will determine whether there are different spatial possibilities. With all three in hand we may then ask whether the answers to arbitrary questions about objects are determined by the way the world is.

According to Q, an object is just the content of a (fully occupied) region of spacetime. But there are two available interpretations of this idea, one rather natural, the other rather less so. The natural reading takes the content of a region to be the object independently of the region it occupies. In effect it presupposes that the identity of some matter ('content') does not depend on where it is. The other reading makes the region 'essential' to the identity of the object (but without necessarily making it a *part* of the object).[17] It leaves no room (as it were) for the content—the object—to have occupied a different region. Of course this conflicts with our everyday conviction that a given object might have been somewhere else. But we have already seen that not all everyday notions have to be respected in serious metaphysics. For example we've already departed from everyday talk in adopting perdurance. But there is also some serious metaphysics that seems to recommend the natural reading while conceding that the identity of an object has *something* to do with spatiotemporal facts. I'll discuss it against the background of QP.

It is a very respectable and common view, and a cornerstone of modern physics, that all matter is composed of 'elementary' or 'fundamental' particles.[18] But on convention QP, this view cannot be quite right as stated. The problem is that the cornerstone view is stated against an unspoken background of intuitive endurantism. So suppose we conceive of fundamental particles as thin spacetime worms in accordance with QP. Then ordinary objects are not literally composed of entire such particles, but rather by proper parts of them. Moreover, and likewise, the instantaneous temporal slices ('stages') and longer proper temporal segments of fundamental particles themselves (and sums thereof, etc.) have no such particles as literal parts, yet they are surely matter and so are also among the Q-objects. Further, it is reasonable to think that particle-worms are not 'point-thin'—that their slices have proper parts. (The reason is that it is hard to conceive of

[17] This point of view is developed in detail in Heller (1990).
[18] Such particles might ultimately be seen as packets (or very local fields) of energy, or modifications of spacetime itself, etc. These details don't matter here.

their having the special roles they do in physical theory while lacking internal structure of one sort or another.) But the proper parts of the stages are also Q-objects and they have no parts that are fundamental particles either (nor do sums of such parts of stages, etc.). So from the perspective of QP, it would be much better to say not that all matter is *composed of* fundamental particles, but rather that all matter is *dependent on* fundamental particles (by being composed of *parts* of fundamental particles). The more 'exotic' Q-objects I've just been describing are surely matter, and their existence in every case clearly depends on the existence of some specific fundamental particles, so let's accept this friendly revision. Thus we may say that all matter is (*fundamental-*) *particle-dependent* (or *particle-based*).

We certainly have a good deal of evidence that this is the way things actually happen to be. But our evidence is incomplete and one might reasonably ask whether things had to be this way even if they are. Might there have been matter without fundamental particles? Or might some matter be particle-based, other not? I am inclined to think that these are genuine possibilities, and will try to accommodate them in developing at least a partial view about the identities of objects. To do this I will need to assume that non-particle-based matter would nevertheless come in various fundamental 'types'. The smallest possible objects of these types may be thought of as non-particle-based *fundamental objects*, and here we should not rule out the possibility of point-thin fundamental objects. They would differ from fundamental particles intrinsically, with their internal physical features somehow failing to rise to *particle* status. Larger non-particle-based objects might consist of stages of such fundamental objects, or sums of such, etc. So let us now extend this list of types by adding types for fundamental particles, so that fundamental particles are just a special variety of *fundamental objects*. Then particle-based objects would either be composed of particle-stages or else would be 'exotic' in one of the ways indicated above. There is of course no good reason for assuming that there could not be some specific matter that was partly particle-based and partly not.

Now let's imagine that we have a (possibly infinite) ultimate list of different fundamental types of matter, including types for all possible fundamental objects, whether particles or not. We may assume that many types on the list are uninstantiated. The 'types' are just properties whose instances we would think of as material spacetime worms (generally very thin). (We should of course not rule out the possibility of *instantaneous* fundamental objects and we'll return to it later. An instantaneous object may be thought of as a degenerate case of a worm—a worm of length zero.) It might prove a little more convenient to idealize this picture by reconfiguring the list so that the instances of all of the types would be worm-shaped *regions* of spacetime. The original list, of course, might have included both properties of matter and properties of spacetime. The idealized reconfiguration would then just amount to replacing the properties that apply properly to matter by surrogate properties of regions.[19] The result would be a fully uniform list of types. But in practice I will continue to speak intuitively of fundamental objects.

Now, what is it to be an object of a fundamental type? I will assume, I think plausibly, that this is a strictly *intrinsic* affair—that such a property is instantiated by an object just in virtue of how that object is in itself. I also assume, again I think reasonably, that no two objects of the same fundamental type have any relevant intrinsic differences.[20] A consequence is that

---

[19] Perhaps as simple as: 'being occupied by a fundamental object of such and such (original) type'.

[20] I say *relevant* because some differences might be viewed as intrinsic but without effecting a difference of type. (Duration may be a good example.) Thus a more refined statement might be that there are no intrinsic differences between stages of fundamental objects of a given type.

being a *specific* fundamental object must be a complex property that is partly intrinsic, reflecting the fundamental type, but also partly relational since the intrinsic features don't distinguish one such object from another. I think there is no real alternative but to take the relational component to be spatiotemporal—it's just too hard to see how it could be anything else. Assuming this, one option (conforming to Mark Heller's 1990 conception) would be to take the relational parameter to be the specific region the worm occupies (during its entire career), thus adopting for these objects the less natural construal of Q. Since arbitrary Q-objects are sums either of stages of fundamental objects or of parts of such stages, the identity of a given object would be derived from the identities of its constituent fundamental-object stages and parts thereof, and we would be stuck with the less natural reading across the board. But I think there is a more satisfying alternative. Speaking loosely, the idea is to view the 'origin' of a fundamental object as essential while keeping its subsequent spatiotemporal history contingent. Then we may hope to derive the identities of arbitrary Q-objects from those of the fundamental objects parts of which go to constitute the Q-objects.

Let's try to develop this in some detail. To begin, notice that there are three ways for any given fundamental object-worm to originate: (1) it may have its origin at some instantaneous spacetime region; (2) it may originate *immediately after* some instant of time, so that it would exist over a 'left-open' continuum whose left limit is that instant of time (but would have no part existing at that instant); and (3) it may be 'backwards-eternal'.[21] For the first case, suppose the given worm has (instantaneous) spacetime origin R. The idea, then, is that to be that *particular* worm is *to be an object of such and such*

---

[21] In what follows I will assume a classical perspective. Adapting it to conform to typical understandings of quantum theory would require probabilistic complications.

fundamental type originating at spacetime region R.[22] This fixes the origins of fundamental objects but leaves their subsequent spacetime careers open (within the limits of spatiotemporal continuity). I believe this 'anti-haecceitist' position is intuitively correct. Two fundamental objects of the same type could *not* have had their spacetime origins interchanged, and as a result they could not have had their (total) spacetime locations interchanged.

The second and third cases are trickier but they yield to essentially the same treatment. First, for any given type T of fundamental object, there is a definite class of regions of spacetime that are suitable for (precisely) containing an object of type T. We call such regions *T-paths*. (Most of them are of course not occupied by T-objects.) Now consider the relation that one T-path bears to another if there is some time prior to which they entirely coincide. Such paths are called *origin-indistinguishable*.[23] Origin-indistinguishability is an equivalence relation, so it partitions the class of all T-paths into equivalence classes. Each equivalence class is, in effect, the set of all possible spacetime histories for a *specific* object of type T. Given that the equivalence classes each contain more than a single path, we automatically depart from the less natural reading of Q. Thus we may think of each equivalence class as a specific *origin-property* for a 'possible T-object'. To be a given T-object,

---

[22] Might more than one object of fundamental type T have originated at the same region R, so that R is fully occupied by matter and there are two 'T-paths' emanating from and including R? It seems to me that we should be disinclined to think this. Although T-objects in general are thin worms, they are generally not worms whose slices are point-objects. We will be inclined to think that what might initially look like a common-origin case is really a case, described intuitively, in which some of the stuff in R 'persists' along one path and the rest of it 'persists' along the other. On the other hand, in the case of point-thin worms, should there be such, we may simply regard one path as having origin R and the other as having an origin left-open to (the time of) R. (An alternative might be to regard the matter at R as an instantaneous 'spawner' with both subsequent paths left-open in origin.)

[23] Paths are *origin-distinguishable* if for any time t, there is a prior time t* such that the t*-slices of the paths are distinct.

then, is to have the property of *being of type T and having such and such origin-property*. The second conjunct is, in effect, the property of *having a path belonging to such and such equivalence class*. So, as we are now thinking, a given T-object might have had a very different spacetime history, but could not have had left-open-to-a-limit or backwards-eternal differences from its actual history. This approach thus adapts the idea of the essentiality of fundamental object origins to the second and third cases.[24] In all three cases, then, a fundamental object might have had different spacetime locations, but never a different 'origin'. Now let's just assume that the equivalence classes of T-paths are *not* unit sets, so that a given such object really might have occupied a different spacetime region.

We now turn our attention to typical objects of everyday acquaintance. These are just aggregations of non-initial segments of fundamental objects (presumably particles), so a given such object could have been in an entirely different spacetime region. The present metaphysical picture of matter therefore comports nicely with the more natural reading of Q, and I will adopt it in what follows. In this picture, a typical ordinary object is a spacetime worm consisting of specific matter composed of temporal stages of specific fundamental objects arranged in a certain complicated way.[25] This matter inherits its specificity, in a way we will now detail, from that of the fundamental object stages that comprise it.

We have already explicitly given the identities of the fundamental objects by exploiting their origins. Now we add that to be a specific *stage* of a specific fundamental object is to be *the most inclusive part of that object that exists at a given time t*.

---

[24] Notice also that our treatment enables us to speak of what are intuitively 'merely possible' fundamental objects (for our given spacetime) without lapsing into Meinongianism or appealing to uninstantiated 'haecceities' or 'individual essences'.

[25] Since segments longer than stages are just sums of stages, we need not treat them explicitly.

This is the entire 't-slice' of the fundamental object, with t the specific instant of time in question, and we may also call it the *t-stage* of the object. This treatment has the consequence, anticipated earlier, that a given stage of a fundamental object *could not* have existed at any time other than the one at which it actually exists. Needless to say, this in no way restricts its spatial location. Finally, since *ordinary* objects are just sums of stages of fundamental objects, we may give their identities by saying that to be a specific such object is to be the sum of such and such specific stages. Its identity as a *certain* mass of matter is rooted in the origins of the fundamental particles whose stages are among its parts. This is true even though the 'origin' of the ordinary object itself is generally far later in time than are those of the fundamental particles some of whose stages are implicated in its identity. Those particles originated long before the earliest stages of the object.

This treatment of the identities of ordinary objects obviously extends to any objects at all that are sums of fundamental object stages. So it extends to all Q-objects save those that were called exotic above. But the characteristic feature of the exotic objects is that they have parts that are proper parts of stages of fundamental objects, but without having the entire stages as parts. So what we need now are plausible identities for proper parts of fundamental particle stages. On our understanding of Q, any object is a sum of point-objects, so our problem reduces to that of saying what it is to be a specific point-object. Our wedge into the problem is that all point-objects are parts of fundamental objects, whose identities reflect their origins as we have detailed.

In fact all point-objects are parts of fundamental object stages, so it will have to emerge that the *time* at which a point-object exists is essential to it. Our problem is now to say what gives a point-object part of a stage its specific identity. We cannot rest the matter on its spatiotemporal location, for this would jeopardize the natural understanding of Q. It must remain possible for that point-object to have been elsewhere at that time.

There are two different assumptions one might make to seal the identities of the point-objects. One would be to assume that for any fundamental object o, and for any point-object p, part of o, there is a unique point-thin path containing p such that the sum of the paths of all of the point-objects in o is precisely the path of o. Then we may introduce the concept of a *fundamental point-object path*, and proceed by analogy with our approach to the identities of fundamental objects. To be a specific point-object would be to be a point-object on a path with a specific 'origin'. An alternative would be to focus on the stage of which a point-object is a part and assume that the point-objects comprising the stage could not have had different relative positions within the stage. Then to be a specific point-object would be to be part of a stage of a specific fundamental object and to occupy such and such specific relative position within that stage.

I'm not entirely happy with either of these approaches, but I may have overlooked a more convincing alternative. In any event, it would by now be very odd to think that we have the identities of fundamental objects and their stages well in hand, but that the point-objects that comprise them do not have specific identities. Moreover, it is difficult to imagine that our larger purpose of analyzing ordinary modal claims about ordinary macroscopic objects might fall victim to a problem about exotic proper parts of fundamental objects. I will therefore assume that we may speak meaningfully of the identities of arbitrary Q-objects, and that their identities always reflect the origins of the fundamental objects on which they depend. We may call the now three-fold package of conventions governing the concept of *object* 'QPO'.[26]

---

[26] Although I believe the fundamental-objects picture is compelling and will proceed as if it is true, one need not adopt it in order to advocate the more

Let's notice how the fundamental objects picture deals with a couple of variations on the familiar example of the qualitatively indistinguishable globes, which we owe to Max Black (1952). One variation involves supposing that we did have a pair of qualitatively indistinguishable globes at a given time and asking whether their spatial positions might have been interchanged. On the present view the answer must be affirmative. The reason is that they are composed of different matter because they are composed of stages of fundamental objects all of whose counterparts between the globes have different origins. Another variation, closer to Black, would be to imagine that the globes suddenly pop into existence *ex nihilo* (and even that they are the only physical objects in the universe). If we are simply considering the first instantaneous stage of their existence, should there be one, then evidently *they* could *not* have been interchanged, for the origins of their fundamental objects would be determined by the very spatiotemporal locations of the initial globe stages themselves. But later stages of the globes could have been interchanged, and for the same reason that was given in the first variation. (And arbitrary stages could have been interchanged in the left-open-to-a-limit case.) Such stages are composed of different matter as a result of their fundamental-object stages' being parts of fundamental objects with different origins.

This is also a good moment to reflect on the debate between proponents of 'stuff-based' and 'thing-based' ontologies of the physical. As I hope the discussions of Q have made clear, there is a certain—very mild—sense in which I don't think the physical world comes with ready-made *objects*. In this sense, I think instead that we (conventionally) carve it up into objects, and that this can be done any way we like. This might sound

---

natural reading of Q. What is required is roughly just that we view any typical matter as having its identity or particularity independently of its actual spatial location. This could be achieved with 'haecceities', for example, but perhaps also in other ways.

The Identities of Objects

like a declaration in favor of stuff as the fundamental category of physical ontology, but I don't intend it that way because there is a crucial twist that rules out that characterization. To adopt Q is to speak of any stuff at all (past, present, or future) as an object (or thing). Moreover, and *from the standpoint of Q*, any such *object* is one that was already there before anyone adopted Q. Since the alleged rivals are stuff and *things*, from the present convention-oriented perspective the debate cannot even be intelligibly framed unless some convention or other about *things* (*objects*) is already in place. And with Q in place, stuff and things are on an entirely even footing. Any stuff—(mass quantifier!)—is a thing, and any thing is just some stuff.

No doubt some proponents of a 'thing-based ontology' have thought that fundamental particles (or objects) are given in nature *as things*, and that since all matter is made of (parts of) these particles, *stuff* is to that extent less fundamental than things. This is to assume that certain things that are ordinarily acknowledged by physics-aware speakers are indeed given and play a fundamental role in the composition of all physical stuff. Charitably understood, this is beyond dispute. From the present perspective, however, such a view presupposes a *convention* under which certain types of stuff are things, which of course is compatible with going the full distance to convention Q, but also compatible with stopping well short. Still, given this, we once again have the twist. For any fundamental particle is surely some stuff and, under the convention, any stuff of that type is a thing. So the stuff of any fundamental particle and the fundamental particle are one and the same (and always have been). If there remains any matter that doesn't count as a thing on such a view, then that merely means the convention stops short of Q.

Under Q there is no *ontological* distinction between stuff and things. The idea that one such category of physical reality could be more fundamental than the other is an illusion because *stuff* and *things* are not distinct categories of reality in the first place. The only genuine distinction in this neighborhood is between different logico-grammatical devices for speaking about the contents of the physical world.[27]

Many have debated whether modality is embedded in the world or is somehow our own conceptual projection onto the world. It is an indisputable fact that we ordinarily think objects persist through time by enduring. But we have seen that thinking this way is not mandatory, and in fact have concluded that for the purposes of metaphysics and semantics it may be better to abandon this ordinary way of thinking. We have also seen that there really does seem to be a 'fact of the matter' as to whether things persist by enduring or by perduring, a fact beyond our detection. In making this decision we commit ourselves to modal views that may in fact be false precisely because modality is embedded in the world in a different way. For this reason we tried to have it both ways by thinking of the perdurance convention in a provisional, conditional way, leaning on the assumption of the ultimate intertranslatability (short of complete details) of the two basic conceptions.

It is also true that we ordinarily think objects could have been located elsewhere, and in developing the QPO package we took pains to accommodate this thinking. Is there a way to view this in strict analogy with the persistence decision, so that there is an undetectable 'fact of the matter' and our convention carries no real metaphysical risk? I think there is, but with the convention of course running the opposite way. We ordinarily think an object could have been elsewhere because we think the physical forces acting on it might have been different. We think a sudden gust of wind might have altered the path

---

[27] See the discussion in Sider (2001: xvi–xx) for a different point of view. The disagreement traces to fundamentally different conceptions of the status of objectual quantification as noted earlier.

of a bird in flight. On this way of thinking, a point-object o within the bird's body might have occupied a different position. But just as we were able to imagine the point-object p (of Section 3) failing to endure along the p–p* path, so that p was distinct from p*, so may we imagine that passing over *space* results in a *different* 'movie-like' replacement of o by a distinct, qualitatively indistinguishable o* at a later time t, not only distinct from o, but also distinct from the point-object that would have been at the relevant place at t on any different path across a stretch of space.[28]

Put abstractly, we are able to imagine four-dimensional 'object-variability', so that it is not just the passing of time that produces new matter in the manner of the 'movie' analogy, but also intuitive 'passing through' space. A better way of putting it might be this. We are able to imagine that point-objects (of various types, perhaps) are the basic material of the physical universe and that, for example, fundamental particles are just special sorts of sums of such objects. Moreover, we can see these point objects as degenerate worms, with their origins (and so their entire locations) essential to their identity. An intuitively enduring stationary point-object at a given position, on this conception, is really a stream of qualitatively indistinguishable point-objects. The same point-object, had it been in intuitive motion starting from the same position, would have been a stream entirely different from the stationary stream save for the starting point-object. Further, had it moved intuitively along any different path, it would have been yet another stream entirely different from any other such stream, again except for the starting point-object.

I have painted a picture of movie-like replacement governing intuitive motion that mirrors the picture of movie-like

---

[28] This conception fits nicely with the idea of matter as 'crimped' spacetime. A different piece of spacetime, however indistinguishable from another, is still a different piece.

replacement governing intuitive persistence. In QPO we have opted for the latter but not the former. By not adopting the former we are sticking with our ordinary thinking about motion and alternative possible location. That both conceptions are available to us suggests that there really is a fact of the matter, but one that is as inaccessible to us in the location case as it is in the persistence case. Thus I suggest that we have another opportunity for a no-fault convention. QPO may be literally incorrect as a description of how the world works, but if it is we know exactly how to fix it, and so we may adopt the same provisional and conditional attitude we adopted in the persistence case. We need a way to speak about the world. We may see QPO as giving us a way that is conveniently precise, but ultimately uncommitted one way or the other (on either front). QPO, while indeed a convention, does not appear to involve any ultimate conceptual imposition on the world. The modal facts about persistence and location are there in the world. We just have to pretend that they go some one of four conceivable ways in order to be able to talk coherently about them. I believe QPO is the most reasonable of the four choices.

6. Mereological Essentialism

The main conclusion of Section 5 was that any matter at all, that is, any object at all, has a definite identity which, with the exception of instantaneous original stages of fundamental objects (and mereological sums thereof), is independent of where it happens to be located in space. This perspective carries with it a commitment to the metaphysical doctrine of mereological essentialism (ME). The reason is that the identity of an object is fixed by the identities of the fundamental-object stages (or, in exotic cases, the point-objects) that are among its parts. What gives a fundamental-object stage (or point-object) its identity is the origin property of its containing fundamental object. Any supposed 'change of parts' of an arbitrary object would involve the addition or subtraction of such stages (or point-objects), and so would result in an object with a different identity—a different object. The parts of an object, specifically the fundamental-object stages (point-objects), determine exactly what object it is. Different parts, different object. In modal terms, the parts of an object are essential to it. No object might have had different parts.

This doctrine has often been rejected on the grounds that it conflicts with common sense about everyday objects. For example, speaking intuitively and without perdurance, we certainly don't think that if we had clipped a toenail of a dog the result would have been a (numerically) different dog. (This is because we're on the familiar-kind side of the great divide. We're thinking about an object as a *dog*.) But examples like this are entirely compatible with ME. To think they are not is to be willing to make what are object-fixated inferences, in this case to infer that it would have been the same *object* from the premise that it would have been the same *dog*. Avoiding the fixation leaves wide open the possibility that a *different* physical object would have been 'the same dog' and so leaves ME untouched. From the standpoint of Q, and still speaking intuitively and without perdurance, there would have remained an object consisting of the discarded clipping and the surviving dog. But this object would not have been a dog at all. It would have been the mereological sum of a dog and an object that was not a part of any dog. Continuing intuitively, the overall situation is best conceived as follows. Every dog (etc.) is a *specific* dog, and for each there is a definite property of being that specific dog. Such a property is instantiated by different objects at different times and also by different objects in different counterfactual situations, and this is exactly what is going on in the examples.[29] This diagnosis will be elaborated in Chapter 4 when we speak more carefully about properties like being such and such dog.

In the meantime there are simpler conceptual reasons favoring ME. What underlies them is the physical-object/parts side of the great divide, which is of course reprised in the more natural interpretation of Q that we adopted with QPO. So I believe this part of the divide reflects a commitment to ME in our everyday concept of a physical object. If this is right, then to reject ME on the object-fixated basis just discussed would be to abandon that concept in favor of one covertly involving associations with familiar kinds.

Let us try to see how our ordinary concept of object supports ME. Here it is important to keep firmly in mind that ME is a principle explicitly about arbitrary *objects* (whether held in company with Q or under some narrower convention about objects).[30]

So let's try a simple 'essentialist'-style thought experiment. Imagine some arbitrary matter (that counts as an object under Q or any prevailing narrower convention). Here, in accordance with ME as a fully general principle about objects, we do not know whether this particular matter is a dog, etc., or an object of any familiar kind at all. Now try to imagine a situation in which that very matter exists, but without some of it existing. Surely any sincere and careful effort to achieve this must fail. The best we can do is to imagine some of the given matter existing without the rest of it existing. And this is simply not to imagine the original matter existing.

---

[29] Restating these points from the perdurantist perspective is no less intuitive, just a bit more cumbersome.

[30] Insofar as dogs (etc.) are objects, it applies to dogs, but not to dogs *qua* dogs. The *object* that is in fact a given dog could not have had different parts. But *that* object need not have been a dog at all. Its parts might have been arranged so that it was not a dog, not an animal, etc., and some *other* object might have had the property of being that particular dog.

Mereological Essentialism

This reflection has a striking consequence under Q. Since no *matter* could have existed without all of it existing, no *physical object* could have existed without all of its parts existing, for each of its parts is just some of its matter. (Of course, none of this is to say that the matter—that is, the object—could not have had a different configuration: that it could is the physical-object/arrangement side of the divide.) I think this simple thought experiment establishes ME (for physical objects) as firmly as any thought experiment could establish any metaphysical thesis, though of course it does so only in company with a convention like Q, so that we may make the transition from the matter to the thing.

How could one reject this thought experiment while retaining, say, Q? To do so, I believe, would be to commit oneself to a fundamentally mysterious conception of the parts of things. On this conception a thing may, under unspecified conditions, (modally) gain or lose parts while retaining its 'identity'. But it's very difficult to entertain such a view coherently without relying unwittingly on ME. For suppose someone claims that an actual object, X, with actual proper part P, could have failed to have P as a part. What could support such a claim? Is it that we can imagine the actual thing $X - P$ (call it 'Z') existing, and then somehow think of it as being X? It's hard to see an alternative, but this can't work. For if an arbitrary thing like X is supposed to be capable of having different parts, then its parts, notably Z and P, must also be capable of having different parts. Thus how do we know that the *actual* thing Z, in the *imagined* situation, wouldn't have P as a part? The only obvious and general way to insure that it wouldn't would be to assume covertly that *in the imagined situation* both the actual Z and the actual P would have the parts they *actually* have! In other words, the only clear and completely general way of achieving the desired outcome would be to presuppose ME. (Of course for the opponent of ME, the fact that P isn't *actually* a part of Z is officially irrelevant, and calling Z 'X – P' in the *imagined* situation would simply beg the question.)

An opponent of ME owes us a completely general account of the conditions under which *objects* (or *matter*) could have been constituted by different parts (or matter). To be plausible, such an account would have to coincide with pre-theoretic intuitions about the modally negotiable parts of objects of familiar kinds like dogs, but would have to do so without invoking such kinds in the effort since ME is merely about objects '*qua* objects', not about objects *qua* arbitrary familiar kinds. This is a very daunting project since our pre-theoretic intuitions about the kinds vary considerably in their stringency from kind to kind. For example we seem to have very conservative intuitions about objects of some kinds (say a Stradivarius) and very liberal ones about others (say the 12th green at Augusta National). A dissenter from ME would have to give a general account that applied to objects of all manner of familiar kinds. But this seems impossible, for often an object of one kind could have been reconfigured so as to be of a different kind, and where the intuitive standards of part-essentiality differed between the two kinds (for example, consider a Rodin and a birdbath).

2
ABSTRACT ENTITIES

1. Face Value

DAVID Lewis offered the following well-known argument in favor of 'possible worlds':

> It is uncontroversially true that things might have been otherwise than they are. I believe, and so do you, that things could have been different in countless ways. But what does this mean? Ordinary language permits the paraphrase: there are many ways things could have been besides the way they actually are. On the face of it, this sentence is an existential quantification. It says that there exist many entities of a certain description, to wit 'ways things could have been'. I believe that things could have been different in countless ways; I believe permissible paraphrases of what I believe; taking the paraphrase at face value, I therefore believe in the existence of entities that might be called 'ways things could have been': I prefer to call them 'possible worlds'.[1]

There are more problems with this argument than we can consider here.[2] I think the most fundamental is that there are three reasonable ways to understand 'things' in this passage, and none of them supports Lewis's ultimate idea that 'ways things could have been' should be seen as *possible worlds*. The three readings that come to mind are *objects*, *states of affairs*, and *the world*. But on any of these, and agreeing with Lewis

---

[1] Lewis (1973: 84).   [2] Some are discussed in Jubien (1988).

to reify, *ways things could have been* would be *properties*, not possible worlds—they would be properties that objects, states of affairs, or the world itself might have had but in fact do not.[3] So the argument gives no convincing reason for favoring an ontology including 'possible worlds'.[4] But, and essentially for this very reason, it does give a 'face value' case in favor of *properties*. Of course we could make such a case independently of counterfactual reflections. Ordinary language is so saturated with apparent reference to and quantification over properties that examples are unneeded. But should we take our property talk at face value?

In the last half of the twentieth century comparatively few analytic philosophers were very comfortable with properties (though there was over these years a growing acceptance). I believe the discomfort traced directly to a certain argument of Quine's, which will be discussed later. Ironically, one of the central explicit goals of *Word and Object* was to find surrogates for properties,[5] relations, and propositions. This goal was important because Quine never hesitated to acknowledge the great utility such posits would have in philosophy, linguistics, and elsewhere.[6] The roles they would play are roles that crucially need playing, which is no doubt why they seem to be so embedded in the ontology of ordinary language in the first place. And this in turn is why the face-value argument is much deeper than a mere appeal to superficial fashion in everyday speech. Properties have central roles to play and we speak every day as if they are playing them right there

---

[3] Robert Stalnaker (1976) made a similar point. No doubt others have made it too.

[4] Possible worlds will be discussed in detail in Chapter 3.

[5] Quine's preferred term is 'attributes'.

[6] Quine says, for example, 'The words "attribute" and "relation" turn up so often in the best discourse on the best of subjects that one may be taken aback by talk of renouncing attributes and relations' (1960: 210). And in Quine (1969: 21) we find: 'There is no denying the access of power that accrues to our conceptual scheme through the positing of abstract objects'.

on center stage. As long as there are no genuine problems with properties, we should welcome them as entirely sensible theoretical posits.

But Quine insisted that all manner of 'intensional entities' have an unsatisfactory 'identity concept' (or 'identity criterion', or 'identity conditions') or none at all, and it is difficult to overestimate the influence this claim has enjoyed. Indeed, it is still widely accepted that the positing of *any* sort of entities at all should be accompanied by a statement of their identity conditions—even entities whose existence is not really in question (like *persons*). But in Section 3 I will argue that this rests on the faulty (or incoherent) presupposition that entities actually *have* variety-specific 'identity conditions' in the first place, so that Quine's argument poses no genuine problem for the positing of properties. But first we will turn briefly to the very notion of a theoretical posit.

2. Posits

In a further (but milder) irony, the natural place to turn for illumination on this topic is the work of Quine himself, who held an utterly reasonable and naturalistic view of posits. On this view the term 'theoretical posit' would actually be redundant because for Quine all talk of existence is ultimately rooted in theory. This emerges very clearly in the closing pages of the famous essay 'On What There Is', where he urges that '[o]ur acceptance of an ontology is...similar in principle to our acceptance of a scientific theory...'[7] He makes it clear that from this perspective even *physical objects* should be seen as posits as opposed to things *given*: 'Physical objects are postulated entities which round out and simplify our account of the flux of experience, just as the introduction

---

[7] Quine (1953, 1961, 1980: 16).

of irrational numbers simplifies laws of arithmetic' (18). That we intuitively view physical objects as if they were given is just a powerful evolutionary inheritance from the prehistory of our species—they are nevertheless entities we postulate to account for and unify our experience, for in no reasonable sense are they given.

In the Foreword to the 1980 re-publication of *From a Logical Point of View* Quine insists that '[p]osited objects can be real' and reiterates that '[t]o call a posit a posit is not to patronize it'.[8] So both physical objects and irrational numbers are posits. If there is any difference of status between different posits it isn't a matter of ontology since all ontology is theory (or theory-embedded). Any difference is epistemic. Thus physical objects might be seen as less fundamental from the phenomenalistic perspective of 'sense-data'; and the irrationals less so from the perhaps more immediately compelling perspective of the (albeit more cumbersome) theory of rational numbers. But no posit is or is not fundamental in itself.

We thus have a view according to which the ultimate test of a posit is the ultimate test of the theory or theories in which it is embedded, and that test, in a word, is *utility* in serving the needs for which the theory was developed. To the extent to which a given theory serves these needs better than its competitors, that theory—and its companion ontology—is to be preferred, at least until something better comes along. That is the way of science and naturalistic philosophy, and we have no better way. This is a sensible picture into which the actual history of science seems to fit nicely. Physical theories 'evolve' and sometimes supplant one another, and scientific ontology can

---

[8] *Op. cit.*: 22. There he added, 'Everything to which we concede existence is a posit from the standpoint of a description of the theory-building process, and simultaneously real from the standpoint of the theory that is being built. Nor let us look down on the standpoint of the theory as make-believe; for we can never do better than occupy the standpoint of some theory or other, the best we can muster at the time'.

change with these changes. With all of its (welcome) vagueness, let's endorse this way of looking at the matter.

In section V of 'Speaking of Objects',[9] Quine comes to grips with attributes—properties—and propositions. He explicitly avows that our conceptual scheme gains significant power if we posit such 'intensional' entities. He claims that some of this power may be gained by positing *classes* instead of properties and propositions, but urges that classes have a 'crystal-clear identity concept' where properties and propositions do not (21). He then explicitly mentions certain advantages the intensional posits would have over classes. For example, rabbit-hunting does not seem to be a relation between a hunter and the class of all rabbits, but rather a relation between a hunter and the property of being a rabbit. Quine adds that '... if attributes clamor for recognition as objects of the attributary attitudes, so do propositions as objects of the propositional attitudes: believing, wishing, and the rest'. He continues:

> Overwhelmed by the problem of identity of attributes and propositions, however, one may choose to make a clean sweep of the lot, and undertake to manage the attributary and propositional attitudes somehow without them. Philosophers who take this austere line will perhaps resort to actual linguistic forms ... as objects of the ... attitudes. (22).

Quine then relates a well-known (and many think persuasive) argument against the viability of linguistic forms for these roles. The argument is the familiar one from Church and Langford based on interlinguistic translation, but Quine claims incomplete satisfaction with it because it appears to depend on 'sameness of meaning'. Finally, he *sympathizes* with the further criticism that resorting to linguistic forms as attitudinal objects is 'discouragingly artificial' (22).

Thus it is difficult to think that Quine himself would not have *preferred* positing properties and propositions over classes were

---

[9] Quine (1969: 21–5).

it not for the alleged problem about identity. Indeed, he is so impressed with the power of properties and propositions that he even contemplates the possibility of finessing the perceived identity problem by making adjustments in logic in order to retain them. Or positing them, mindful of the problem, for *some* theorizing (which he calls 'second-grade') while reserving theories with less dicey posits for 'official scientific business', abandoning the ideal of a single universal system so as to make room for them (23–4).

Thus only the supposed problem of identity stood between Quine and the positing of properties. He had exactly the same sorts of theoretical reasons for positing properties as for physical objects, atoms and molecules, and numbers, and he had explicit misgivings about positing surrogates to play the roles of properties. So let's look at the alleged identity problem.

3. Identity Conditions

Quine's criticism of intensional entities is that they lack a clear 'identity concept' (or 'criterion' or, as it is more typically put today, 'identity conditions'). Underlying this criticism is the more general idea that if one posits entities of any kind, one should accompany the positing with a statement of clear identity conditions *for entities of that supposed kind*. But even if we assume that entities of various kinds have identity conditions, there remains something immediately suspicious about the idea that these conditions should vary from kind to kind. Intuitively, there is just *one* relation of identity. When we say that certain numbers are (or are not) identical, we are *apparently* asserting that the same relation holds (or fails to hold) as when we assert that certain physical objects (etc.) are (or are not) identical. We're asserting that the items in question are *just one thing* (or else are two).

Identity Conditions

Thus when we speak carefully of identity we take ourselves to be speaking of a single relation, not of a cluster of different, kind-restricted, identity-like relations whose analyses might vary from kind to kind. If there really were this plenitude of identity-like relations, we would have to wonder what it meant to deny, say, that Julius Caesar and a particular number were identical. But it seems clear that it simply means that Julius Caesar and the number are not a single entity.

So why does Quine, who of course was under no illusions about the relation of identity, find it reasonable to think that whether that relation holds in a given case depends directly on the nature of the objects in question? If we were indeed dealing with a cluster of different kind-restricted relations, it might be plausible to think that each had its own distinctive analysis. But we are not, and it isn't plausible to think that identity, as it applies to objects of different kinds, has correspondingly different analyses. It isn't even clear what this would mean. One would think either that identity is a simple, unanalyzable relation, or else that it has a single analysis, one that prevails across the realms of physical objects, numbers, classes, and even properties or propositions, should such entities exist in the first place.

And why should we think identity has any analysis at all? When seen as the fully general, topic-neutral relation we normally take it to be, it is very odd to think there are any more fundamental concepts in terms of which it could plausibly be analyzed. It is simply far-fetched—even incoherent—to think that, *given an entity*, of whatever kind, its being a *single* entity somehow consists in its satisfying some condition involving the kind to which it belongs (or concepts related to that kind).

Quine appears to acknowledge that some philosophers indeed *have* posited entities like properties and propositions, though *without* having given appropriate identity conditions. But how can it make sense for him to concede this? To claim that there are, for example, properties, is to say that there are certain *individual entities* of a specific sort. The very claim presupposes that any such entity is just itself (and not two or more entities, whatever that could mean). So, officially, Quine should not have conceded that such posits have been made at all, since they would be incoherent in the absence of appropriate identity conditions. But surely such posits have been made, and they are entirely coherent, whether true or false. Either the posited entities, should they exist, satisfy conditions that ground universal, topic-neutral identity, but which we haven't so far been able to state, or else, and much more reasonably, identity is a simple relation not grounded in identity conditions at all.

To be sure, someone who posits entities of a given kind owes us at least a general explanation of what they are supposed to be like. We have to get onto the *kind*, at least to some reasonable extent. We could not seriously take Lewis Carroll as having posited *borogoves* (not that he meant to) merely by telling us that they frequent the *wabe* and at times are *mimsy*. But the proponents of entities like properties and propositions have told us a great deal about what they are supposed to be like and Quine frequently makes it clear that none of this has escaped his notice.

Despite all of this, Quine writes as if identity had multiple analyses, varying from kind to kind, and he offers the principle of extensionality for classes as a paradigm case. Extensionality says that classes are identical if they have the same members. In the language of first-order logic,

$$(x)(y)[(z)(z \in x \leftrightarrow z \in y) \to x = y].$$[10]

Here it is understood that 'x' and 'y' range only over classes (and we could insert explicit quantifier restrictions to that

---

[10] Notice that although extensionality is often stated as a universal *biconditional*, strictly speaking it is not since we get the other direction for free as a consequence of the first-order axioms governing '='.

effect if we wanted). The range of 'z' depends on the specific theory we are considering. In the most wide-open version it would include all classes in its range. (For example this is what happens in pure Zermelo-Fraenkel set theory. In impure theories classes might or might not be included.) For present purposes I will assume that we are looking at a theory in which classes may be members of classes, so that 'z' ranges over all classes. (In this context Quine does not appear to intend 'class' in the sense of the term associated with the two-sorted set/class theory of Gödel and Bernays. He intends it rather in the sense we now commonly reserve for 'set'.)

Now, exactly what should we make of the principle of extensionality? It does give a sufficient condition for arbitrary x and y to be just one class. But this doesn't entail that the identity of x and y *consists in* or even *depends on* their having the same members. There are infinitely many distinct sufficient conditions for the identity of arbitrary x and y. For example, it is sufficient that they be members of exactly the same classes.[11] So it is very misleading to call extensionality an identity concept or to view it as providing identity conditions for classes, as if there were some external relational condition x and y would have to meet *in order to be* just one class. Extensionality is, rather, a principle that partly delineates the *concept of class*. It does so by entailing that if there were entities to which the concept of membership applied, but such that distinct ones might have the same members, then they wouldn't be classes, but rather entities of some other sort.

In fact it is entirely reasonable to think there *are* such entities. I have in mind *ordered sets*. Distinct ordered sets may have precisely the same members and, viewing extensionality as helping characterize the concept of class, this guarantees that they aren't classes. Nowadays it is of course very common to 'identify' ordered sets with (unordered) classes, for example

---

[11] $(x)(y)[(z)(x \in z \leftrightarrow y \in z) \to x = y]$.

in a manner generalized from Kuratowski's 'reduction' of ordered pairs to classes. (<a, b>'=' {{a, b},{a}}.) But I think it cannot be seriously maintained that ordered sets really *are* the classes they are 'identified with' under such a convention. The reason is that order is intrinsic to an ordered set, but its corresponding class under the convention has no intrinsic order. The order is 'coded into' the class, but *we* have to *interpret* the coding for it to generate the order. The coding element does not generate it on its own. So the convention merely provides *surrogates* for ordered sets, not the ordered sets themselves.

Let's pause a moment to consider what Quine might say in response to these claims. One thought is that he might concede that the terms 'identity concept', 'identity criterion', and 'identity conditions' are misleading, and that in saying extensionality gives the identity concept for classes, all he intended was that it partly circumscribes the concept of a class as just suggested. Then the complaint about attributes and propositions would be that these notions had been left too vague, that no general principles like extensionality had been advanced to help us get a grip on them. In effect, the complaint would be that they're somehow *obscure*—more akin to borogoves than to classes.

But it isn't so. It is every bit as distinctive of attributes that more than one of them may have the same instances, as it is of classes that no more than one of them may have the same members (not that instantiation and membership play exactly parallel roles in their respective theories). Certainly no one would think that *ordered sets* are obscure because more than one of them may have the same members, so the parallel complaint about attributes has no bite. Thus one might think that just as extensionality helps delineate the concept of *class*, the failure of the instantiation-analogue of extensionality does the same for *attribute* (as it does for *ordered set*).

Identity Conditions

Of course the notion of extensionality has no literal (and nontrivial) application to attributes in the first place. The theory of classes is the theory of certain posits *along with* a characteristic relation that either holds or fails to hold between pairs of them (and between arbitrary entities and classes). The principle of extensionality explicitly and essentially concerns this relation. To say that attributes are obscure because they're not extensional in *this* sense would thus be a kind of category mistake. Of course attributes do not have members, but neither do the stars and planets. There is indeed a characteristic relation bound up with the notion of attribute, but it isn't membership, it's *instantiation*. Thus we should simply say that it helps circumscribe the concept of attribute to postulate that distinct attributes may have the same instances, in just the way it helps circumscribe the concept of class to postulate extensionality. As a result, reconstruing 'identity concept' (etc.) in the softer way now contemplated doesn't really bolster Quine's case against attributes.

Let's therefore return to the original notion that extensionality is a paradigm case of identity conditions in the sense that it says what is required—what *conditions* must be met—for classes x and y to be identical. I have insisted that the idea that posits of any kind should be held to such a standard should be rejected. But I would like to conclude this section by noting a peculiarity that should disturb even those who might be tempted to accept it.

When Quine casts about for potential candidates for identity conditions for attributes, he does something very odd. In a nutshell, he goes *linguistic* instead of *metaphysical*. Extensionality of course concerns only classes and their members. It isn't about *referring* to classes or the like. Thus it is very surprising when Quine quotes Carnap, who wrote, '... two sentences about x attribute the *same* attribute to x if and only if the two sentences are not merely alike in truth value for each choice of x, but necessarily and analytically so, by sameness of meaning'.[12] Quine quickly rejects this proposal on the grounds that it depends on the 'obscure' notion of *synonymy*. But setting that aside, it is striking that Carnap's formulation would not provide identity conditions in the style of extensionality. What it would instead provide would be a condition for a certain semantic relation (in effect the *expression* relation) to hold between each of *two* linguistic entities (in effect *predicates*) and *one* attribute. Far from giving identity conditions for attributes, this appears to presuppose that identity for attributes is already fully under control. Carnap has in effect given us a candidate for what amounts to an analysis of what might be called the *predicate-co-expression* relation—a relation that holds between pairs of linguistic entities.

Quine never considers candidates for identity conditions for attributes that actually parallel extensionality. This is surprising because there is an obvious candidate (with 'μ' representing instantiation):

$$(x)(y)[(z)(x \mu z \leftrightarrow y \mu z) \rightarrow x = y].$$

It says that attributes are identical if they have the same attributes.[13] I believe it is true. Notice that it quantifies over all attributes just as extensionality (in the pure case) quantifies over all classes. It also exploits the characteristic relation for attributes just as extensionality exploits the characteristic relation for classes. I would say that it provides satisfactory identity conditions for attributes if and only if extensionality provides satisfactory identity conditions for classes. But of course I would deny the latter, and so also the former. There is the general problem, discussed above, of the universality and topic-neutrality of identity, which makes it seem implausible that we need kind-restricted identity conditions in the first

---

[12] Quine (1969: 19) [quoting from Carnap (1947: 23)].
[13] I will later adopt somewhat different notation for instantiation. Here the goal was to parallel extensionality as explicitly as possible.

place. But there is also the more local problem of quantifying over all entities of a given kind in order to give *their* identity conditions. (Singular) quantification is incoherent unless each entity over which the quantifiers range is a specific entity, and so identical with itself and with no other. Quine's famous slogan, 'No entity without identity', should not be understood as an admonition to provide identity conditions when positing, but rather as the truism that any entity is identical with itself, and automatically so. Entityhood and identity are two sides of a single coin.

I believe it was easy for Quine to fix on Carnap's linguistic candidate and overlook metaphysical ones because he was on a virtually obsessive mission to dispense with *meant entities*, and could not even begin to think of attributes without thinking of them as the entities that are posited to be the meanings of predicates. But for Plato, of course, the theory of forms was at bottom a theory about how things are the ways that they are, and surely this conviction is shared by any contemporary property theorist. If properties wind up as meanings, it is a great bonus, a happy adjunct (or corollary) to their playing this more fundamental role. Thus any serious attempt to clarify or circumscribe the notion of attribute must begin with the relation of instantiation, not with linguistic expression.

So it seems to me that Quine's famous objection to attributes (and other intensional entities) does not merit the respect and influence it actually enjoyed. It also seems to me that apart from this ultimately ineffectual objection, Quine himself had every reason to include attributes in his ontology along with physical objects, numbers, and (perhaps) classes, and for essentially the same sorts of reasons. That is what I will be doing in what follows. I believe properties provide the best available tool for understanding the metaphysics of ordinary objects, alethic modality, and the semantics of ordinary language, prominently including proper names, and I hope this claim will gain in plausibility as this book unfolds. It is of course conceivable that these goals might some day be achieved within a more austere ontology. In that event, and in the spirit of Quine's general approach to posits, I would be inclined to prefer it. But at the moment I believe no such rival approach is a serious competitor.[14]

4. About Properties

I will not offer a general theory of properties in this book. One reason is that I don't believe there is any truly natural and intuitive way to do it. Any full-blown theory would have to turn at least somewhat unnatural in order to cope with potential paradox. This was evident in the system of *Principia Mathematica* and, of course, had its parallel in the development of set theory as a branch of mathematics. Intuitive understandings of both properties and sets are inconsistent, and all well-known efforts to remedy this seem one way or another unnatural or even ad hoc. A more important reason for skipping property theory is that it would be an overly technical distraction from our central topics.[15]

Still there are a few assumptions about properties that I will rely on in what follows and I'll begin to mention them now. To begin, I will proceed as if the realm of properties is 'abundant' rather than 'sparse', though I won't enter into the debate between proponents of the two conceptions. As

---

[14] The topics of this section are discussed more fully in Jubien (1996) and (2004).

[15] In fact I think set theory is best thought of as an idealized fragment of property theory. For every set, there are infinitely many properties having that set as their common extension. So set theory may be seen as 'projected' from property theory (roughly) by replacing the axiom that provides for coextensiveness by extensionality. Semantically, we collapse the universe of properties so that for any original property, there remains exactly one from among those having the same instances. Then we view the survivors as *sets* by reconstruing instantiation as membership. If any conception along these lines is adopted, then it is clear that property theory must incorporate devices for avoiding paradox, and these can be no more natural or intuitive than their analogues in set theory.

a practical matter, this means I will write as if there is a property expressed by any of a very wide range of ordinary English predicates. This range includes bizarrely disjunctive predicates like 'is singing in Vienna or made of ice', and bizarrely relational predicates like 'has been thought about by a Romanov on a February 29th'. In admitting 'Cambridge', 'converse intentional', and other weird-seeming properties I take comfort in the following thought. Certainly it might be true that a Romanov thought about (say) the Taj Mahal on a certain February 29th. If there really is such a property, then speaking as if the Taj Mahal instantiated it is of course perfectly appropriate since the instantiation might actually hold. But if the realm of properties is actually sparse and there really is no such property, then the truth of the claim would of course not consist in the contemplated instantiation, but rather in the instantiation of some genuine (sparse) properties by genuine entities. (It might all come down to properties of quarks.) In such a case speaking as if the converse intentional property were instantiated may be viewed as a manner of speaking, an abbreviation of a no doubt unknown conjunction of whatever sorts of sparse instantiations would in fact make for the truth of the original claim. We would have, in effect, a grounding of nonliteral abundant property talk in literal sparse property talk. Thus I feel comfortable in speaking as if the realm of properties is abundant. Once we grant that properties account for the way the world is, we might as well make life easier by pretending there is an abundance of them doing this metaphysical work.

There is a cornerstone principle underlying the Platonic conception of properties that will play a very large role in what follows. According to this principle, for an entity to be a certain way, for example *green*, is nothing more nor less than for it to instantiate a certain property, in this case the property of *being green* (or *greenness*). Thus, for example, Fenway Park's being green is a state of affairs in which a certain concrete entity stands in a certain relation to a certain abstract entity. Someone who says 'Fenway Park is green', then, expresses an intuitive proposition that has an abstract entity, *greenness*, as an intuitive constituent. This everyday utterance thus expresses the same intuitive proposition as would a philosopher's utterance of 'Fenway Park instantiates (the property of) *greenness*'. For want of a better term, I will call this the (Platonic) Principle of Constitution. Properties *constitute* things as being one way or another by having those things as instances. Obviously constitution, in this sense, is not 'active' or 'causal' (or 'explanatory'). What brought it about that Fenway Park is green was certainly not an abstract entity, but rather the activity of some painters. They brought it about that the stadium instantiated *greenness*. But its now being green consists in this instantiation quite independently of how it came to pass.

The Principle of Constitution has an extremely important consequence for the application of symbolic logic in philosophical semantics and in philosophy generally. The consequence is that first-order logic—as it is *typically* applied—does not do justice to the intuitive proposition expressed by a sentence like 'Fenway Park is green'. Since this sentence and 'Fenway Park instantiates *greenness*' are synonymous, and since the latter sentence supports existential quantification on 'greenness', the normal way of 'translating' the former sentence must fall short of expressing the intuitive proposition. It clearly follows from that proposition that there is some property that Fenway Park instantiates. But the *usual* rendering of the first sentence blocks this inference because it 'translates' 'is green' by a predicate letter, and predicate position is immune to quantification in first-order logic.

The remedy I prefer is a formulation in which the instantiation is rendered explicitly and 'is green' is represented by a (quantifiable) singular term. (An alternative, which I won't pursue, would be to abandon first- in favor of second-order logic.) This reform in the application of logic will ultimately help us see that the two sides of the great divide are fully compatible. Along the way we will notice a further, closely related shortcoming in the typical application of logic—one that has clouded our thinking about the topics of proper names and modality.

3

AGAINST POSSIBLE WORLDS

1. Lewis's Analysis of Modality

IN Chapter 4 I will offer an *analysis* of the metaphysical notions of possibility and necessity, and I'll begin this chapter by looking at the best-known existing effort in that direction. That of course is David Lewis's elegant and rather surprising theory of possible worlds and counterparts. It is not likely that many people presently favor Lewis's approach, whether in detail or broadly. I think it is nevertheless important to review it because it embodies a certain structural feature that I believe would undermine *any* proposed analysis of these notions based on 'possible worlds', regardless of how the worlds might be conceived ontologically.

Nowadays it is unusual to overhear a philosophical conversation (on almost any topic) that doesn't make apparent appeals to possible worlds. But only rarely are those who actually rely on worlds prepared to say exactly what they are, that is, to offer an ontological characterization. Some apparent appeals to worlds are of course intended only metaphorically, so that 'There's a world in which …' is just a vivid synonym for 'It's possible that …' Others rely on worlds as genuine entities and explicate them—in different ways—as complex *abstract entities*.[1] Still others make genuine but unexplicated appeals to worlds, as if their existence and nature were unproblematic.

Lewis was refreshingly direct about the matter.[2] He posited, boldly and again surprisingly, that other possible worlds really exist and are entities more or less like the (at least partly) concrete world that we inhabit. And here he stipulated that our world consists of everything at any distance in space and time from us. So any worlds other than ours must be spatiotemporally detached from ours (and from each other) as a matter of sheer stipulation, a point to which we will soon return.

At the time Lewis gave us this conception we were already very much softened up for the general idea that for something to be possible consisted in (or was equivalent to) its being *true in some possible world*. We may think of this as the *fundamental tenet of world theory*. So it appeared to many at the time that the analytic project boiled down to saying first just what possible worlds *are*, and then exploiting them in a semantical analysis ultimately treating both modality *de dicto* and *de re*. The hoped-for result would be a 'reductive' analysis of these modal concepts, where the reducing notions were those of *truth* and the now elucidated ontology of *possible worlds*. Let's begin by thinking briefly just about the postulated worlds, reserving for later the complication of counterparts.

I think those who have been tempted by Lewis's conception of worlds have likely fallen prey to 'persuasive terminology'. They have been seduced by his decision to *call* the postulated realms *possible worlds*, and so have been encouraged to see

---

[1] For example as 'maximal consistent propositions'. Those who treat worlds as abstract entities generally rely on primitive modality in saying just which entities they count as worlds. As a result they typically intend no *analysis* of the modal notions. At the same time we should not rule out in advance the possibility of an analysis based on a conception of abstract worlds not relying on primitive modality. For a discussion of 'abstract' and 'concrete' notions of possible worlds, see van Inwagen (1986).

[2] For example in Lewis (1986: section 1.1).

these realms as relevant to nontrivial possibilities, especially possibilities for things that actually exist. I also think that any further steps one might take to legitimize the possible-worlds terminology would disqualify the proposed analysis as 'reductive'. Let's turn now to these two complaints.

Certainly there might exist what we may neutrally call (*spatiotemporally*) *detached realms*. So suppose there really are such things. Why are they not parts of the world, that is, *our* world? For Lewis they aren't, but only because he has stipulated that our world consists of what is spatiotemporally connected to us. But what could justify this stipulation? Surely it is not the raw intuitive philosophical notion. On that conception *the world* includes *whatever exists*, and since for Lewis the other realms truly do exist, they count intuitively as parts of the world. If there actually are detached realms, the consequence is simply that the physical part of our world is fragmented in this interesting but unobservable way.

I don't doubt that there may be some detached *realms*. Future physicists might even have theoretical reasons for positing them. But if we decide to call them *possible worlds*, we are begging the question of their relevance to our intuitive notion of possibility. For all we know, there might be just two such realms, or twenty-seven, or uncountably many, or even 'set-many'. Suppose there are just a few, but that all of them happen to include stars. How plausible is it to think that if this is how things really are, then we've just been wrong to regard the existence of stars as contingent? Or suppose it happens that there are no other detached realms. Would we happily accept the consequence that we exist necessarily, that we've been overly humble to think we're mere contingent beings? Lewis's proposal was complicated by the presupposition that much of what we normally take to be possible really is possible, so that we would need infinitely many 'worlds' in order to capture our ordinary thinking. But a fully general, strictly analytic proposal would not presuppose this, simply letting the chips fall where they may (as it were) as to whether and how many other 'worlds' exist. Of course if we are reluctant to think, for example, that our existence would be necessary if there were no other realms, we should be just as reluctant to think that our intuitive contingency depends on there being other realms with no people.

If we've already fallen for the idea that the other realms are *possible worlds*, that is, if we're under the spell of the persuasive terminology, then *of course* it will seem that for something to be possible is for it to be true in (or with respect to) at least one of them. That, after all, is the essential *role* of worlds in accordance with the fundamental tenet of world theory. We were already primed for this by the work of modal logicians and philosophers such as Jaakko Hintikka, Saul Kripke, Ruth Barcan Marcus, and Richard Montague.[3] But when we think only of the pure, untitled ontological picture of detached *realms*, other realms seem to have nothing at all to do with our at-home notion of possibility (even if we imagine there are enough realms to generate intuitively correct truth values in a formal semantics). Thus it seems to me that detached realms have a severe problem of *relevance*: they cannot reasonably be thought to be relevant to modality as we typically take it, and their irrelevance was merely veiled by the decision to call them possible worlds.

As claimed above, when we reflect in the terminologically neutral way it seems clear that any other realms that happened to exist would just be scattered parts of the *actual world*, not entire *worlds* at all. They would be actually existing entities. It would just happen that physical reality was structured in this remarkable yet modally inconsequential way. There would be no call for restricting our notion of actuality to the connected realm we happen to inhabit, as Lewis does, nor for viewing the

---

[3] See, for example, Hintikka (1961), Kripke (1963), Marcus (1993), essay 4, and Montague (1974), essays 5 and 6.

other realms each as 'actual' with respect to itself but to the exclusion of the others.

In ordinary talk, 'the world' often just means the earth. This parochial use of the term may in fact be more common than any other. But we philosophers generally use the term in a more cosmopolitan way, in the intuitive philosophical way mentioned above that includes everything that exists. Of course it would also be parochial, only on a grander scale, to presume that all of physical reality is spatiotemporally connected to us. In fact we simply don't know the extent of the world. But if it happens to be a single continuous manifold, it doesn't follow that everything true is necessarily true. All the usual possibilities remain, awaiting roundup by a correct analysis.

Thus it seems to me that Lewis's postulation of concrete 'worlds', when stripped of the persuasive terminology, and even before considering details about 'counterparts', is implausible. I think it's implausible whether we take it as presented, with infinitely many 'worlds', or as a pure analytic proposal, with no commitment as to the quantity of 'worlds'.

Suppose now that this much has been accepted. We might then wonder whether some further (and plausible) metaphysical assumption or strategy might be invoked to render any otherwise irrelevant realms relevant, in effect to elevate them to the status of genuine *worlds*. Thus suppose we resolve to go ahead and postulate detached realms and even to call them possible worlds, but with a strategy in mind to render them relevant to actual possibilities, to make them merit the title. What might such a strategy be like?

Without framing the question quite this way, Lewis provided an answer. We may interpret him as agreeing (as surely he would) that calling the other realms worlds does not make them modally relevant, but then as claiming that what makes them relevant is that some of them contain *counterparts* of entities that exist in our realm. Then the entire package of detached realms and counterparts would be modally relevant, so that in the end the possible-worlds terminology would be fully justified. Lewis wrote:

> Humphrey may be represented *in absentia* at other worlds, just as he may be in museums in this world... The museum can have a waxwork figure to represent Humphrey... Another world... can have as a part... a Humphrey of its own, a flesh-and-blood counterpart of our Humphrey, a man very like Humphrey in his origins, in his intrinsic character, or in his historical role. By having such a part, a world represents *de re*, concerning Humphrey... that he exists and does thus-and-so... [B]y winning the presidential election, the other-worldly Humphrey represents the this-worldly Humphrey... as winning... This is counterpart theory, the answer I myself favour to the question how a world represents *de re*.[4]

And a bit later he added,

> Counterpart theory does say... that someone else—the victorious counterpart—enters into the story of how it is that another world represents Humphrey as winning, and thereby enters into the story of how it is that Humphrey might have won... Insofar as the intuitive complaint is that someone else gets into the act, the point is rightly taken... What matters is that the someone else... should not crowd out Humphrey himself. And there all is well. Thanks to the victorious counterpart, Humphrey himself has the requisite modal property: we can truly say that *he* might have won. (196).

So, in a nutshell, other realms are held to be relevant to this-world possibility because they have parts that *represent* parts of this world as being ways they in fact are not.

But I think there are two important reasons why this cannot work. The first is that it's implausible to claim that Humphrey's other-worldly counterpart *represents* anything of Humphrey simply as a result of being similar to him in this or that respect. The reason is that genuine representation does not take place merely as a result of similarity. For that matter, successful representation does not require any species of similarity in

[4] Lewis (1986: 194).

the first place.[5] What it requires is a certain sort of *intentionality*. In the commonest sort of case a waxwork figure in a museum represents Humphrey because its maker intended it to represent him and because it is presented in the museum as doing so (or, less commonly, because it was an object appropriated to represent Humphrey, or the like). It *wouldn't* (in the normal case) represent Humphrey's long lost identical twin, or his clone, or anyone else physically indistinguishable from Humphrey. Moreover, its representing Humphrey isn't an automatic result either of how it is in itself or of its standing in any specific similarity relation to him. Humphrey's Republican clone would not (automatically) represent Humphrey as being a Republican. An entity—here or in some other realm—may come to represent Humphrey only if someone acts intentionally so as to bring this about. But no one could bring it about that an entity represents Humphrey without being causally connected both to Humphrey and to the entity. So no one in our realm can bring it about that an other-worldly counterpart does this, and neither can anyone in the counterpart's realm. As a result, the concept of *representation* does not give us a wedge into the problem of the modal irrelevance of the other realms.

The second reason the counterparts don't work is this. Suppose, despite what has just been claimed, that some otherworldly person similar to Humphrey *really did* represent Humphrey as winning. Why would it follow from this fact that Humphrey might have won? Surely we can represent things as being ways they could not be. Here is perhaps an example. Many have thought that Kripke (1972, 1980: 110–13) argued persuasively that it is (metaphysically) impossible for Queen Elizabeth II to have been the (natural) daughter of the

---

[5] A spy, using a prearranged signal code, can use a potato chip to represent Humphrey to a confederate (or we can use a sequence of eight letter-tokens beginning with a token of 'H', as I just did).

Trumans (given that in fact she was not). Assuming he was right, this would not prevent someone from staging a play in which she was represented as being the Trumans' daughter.[6] Misrepresentation is not missed representation, but rather a kind of representation.

One way to avoid these problems might be to postulate directly that there exist *genuinely modal properties* such as *making it possible that Humphrey won* and that they are instantiated by other realms (or parts of other realms). But this would be a very suspect approach (involving an independently suspect ontology) for we could simply have postulated at the outset that *Humphrey* has the genuinely modal property of *possibly winning*, thereby saving the elaborate detour through the other realms. Worse, this direct approach would obviously destroy any hope of reductiveness for the analysis and would create a strong suspicion of circularity as well.

There may, of course, be other strategies for providing the right kind of modal oomph for the worlds but without such unhappy consequences. But here it's important to emphasize that any successful strategy, with or without 'counterparts', really must—somehow or other—confer just such *intuitive* modal properties on the various possible worlds. We must see it as appropriate, given such a strategy, to view other worlds as *making it possible that Humphrey won*. We've already seen that calling the other realms possible worlds doesn't achieve this. And we saw just now that the relations that Lewis officially enlists as counterpart relations don't help either.

Seeing things from a slightly different angle, counterpart relations are just more or less stringent similarity relations, describable in strictly nonmodal terms. It simply doesn't follow from A's nonmodal similarity to B (no matter how impressive

---

[6] I recently saw a television advertisement in which it was represented that a young man was seated on a chair near a sofa on which he was sitting. The advertisement (helpfully?) mentioned a 'disruption of the space-time continuum'.

it might be) that A makes something possible *for B*.[7] If someone similar to Humphrey won, that nicely establishes the possibility of someone's winning who is similar to Humphrey. But we mustn't confuse this possibility with the intuitively different possibility of *Humphrey's* winning.[8] For the former to establish the latter a further hypothesis (or presupposition) would be required. Any further hypothesis would, in effect, have to confer upon A an intuitive modal property involving B, and hence would have to be modal in its own right. For this reason I hold that Lewis's analysis, if bolstered so as to establish the other realms as fully fledged, modally relevant *possible worlds*, would not be 'reductive' in the sense of reducing modality to a complex interplay of *nonmodal* concepts. (And for the very same reason, we may now wonder whether we could really regard such a strategy as providing even a *nonreductive* analysis of these modal notions, for it appears to rest on concepts of the very sort it seeks to analyze. But I won't press this point.)

2. Worlds in General

I began by discussing Lewis's proposal mainly because it is so well known. But in fact I think that *any* possible-worlds analysis would be doomed regardless of the intrinsic natures of the postulated worlds, and for reasons that were implicit in the above comments on Lewis. I will be more explicit about these reasons in a moment. But first I want to set a framework for the discussion by recalling the standard semantics of modal logic. I believe the contemporary infatuation with possible worlds in philosophy stems in part from a tendency to think that

---

[7] Kripke (1972, 1980: 45, fn. 13) was apparently thinking along similar lines.
[8] Lewis's remark that 'all is well' on the matter of whether Humphrey's counterpart 'crowd[s] out Humphrey himself' sounds a bit like wishful thinking since Humphrey isn't there and no one who is there can represent him.

technical logic offers silver-bullet solutions to philosophical problems. So let's look at standard modal semantics with the question firmly in mind of how it might be relevant to analyzing modality.

In Kripke's well-known version,[9] a *propositional model structure* is an ordered triple <G,K,R>, where K is a set having G as a member and R (the 'accessibility relation') is a subset of K × K. For our purposes it suffices to simplify by taking R to be all of K × K. The result is that all members of K are relevant to evaluating modal formulas with respect to any member of K. Atomic formulas are assigned truth values with respect to each member of K. Then, by induction on the number of connectives, truth-functionally molecular formulas receive truth values with respect to each member of K. The induction is the familiar one from nonmodal propositional logic, but now carried out with respect to each member of K and the stipulated truth values of the atomics with respect to that member of K. (So, e.g., arbitrary '***A*** & ***B***' receives T with respect to arbitrary H iff both '***A***' and '***B***' receive T with respect to H.) Simultaneously, modal formulas receive truth values inductively with respect to each member of K, with all members of K relevant to the distribution. An arbitrary formula '◊***A***' receives the truth value T with respect to a member H of K iff there is a member H′ of K with respect to which '***A***' receives T. (In the fully general semantics, '◊***A***' receives T with respect to H iff there is some member H′ of K such that <H,H′> is a member of R and '***A***' receives T with respect to H′.)

The key thing to notice about the semantics is that it imposes no restrictions at all on the natures of the members of K. So for any nonempty set you like, there are model structures in which that set serves as K. Such a K may include giraffes, dust motes, spiral galaxies, detached concrete realms, von Neumann ordinals, propositions, or what have you. A

---

[9] As presented, for example, in Kripke (1963).

metaphysical question on which the semantics is neutral is whether there are model structures in which K includes 'merely possible' entities. This question becomes much more pressing when quantifiers are introduced, as we will soon see.

Kripke offered a gloss on the semantics in what I believe was an unfortunate effort to promote intuitive understanding. It was that we may *think of* the members of K as 'possible worlds' and of its distinguished member G as 'the actual (or 'real') world'. If we do think this way we can see that the semantics roughly conforms to (a generalization of) the above mentioned fundamental tenet of world theory: the idea that *for something to be possible is for it to be true in some (appropriate) possible world*. But thinking this way is at least a bit misleading because what the semantics actually does is merely to distribute truth values to formulas *with respect to* 'possible worlds'. The 'in' (or 'at') of the semantics is really just shorthand for 'with respect to' because the semantics says nothing and requires nothing about the intrinsic natures of the possible worlds (that is, the members of K). But this clearly falls short of the natural philosophical construal of the central tenet, where we expect worlds to be such that their internal goings on determine what is possible in the actual world.

So I believe the semantics is better taken for what it really is and without the possible-worlds gloss: it is a strictly *mathematical* device for distributing truth values to formulas with respect to arbitrarily chosen entities (often called 'indices'). It is true that if a modal formula receives the truth value T with respect to (say) G, then it does so (in general) as a consequence of the truth values received by simpler component formulas with respect to indices other than G. But so far this is just mathematics, not modal metaphysics. It is surely fair to say that the mathematics has been crafted in order to deliver a truth value distribution compatible with the central tenet of world theory. But this tenet, intuitive though it might have seemed to those under the influence of the semantics, cannot rise to the status of an analysis of the notion of possibility until we have been told *what the possible worlds are like and why what goes on in other possible worlds has anything to do with what is true in a given possible world.*

The most that might reasonably be claimed at this point, I believe, is that insofar as modal logic, interpreted in this fashion, is taken to bear directly on the intuitive notions of possibility and necessity, these notions are simply being *presumed* to function in accordance with a certain mathematical structure. But the structure has the disturbing feature that modal statements (in general) have their truth values fixed by facts about entities that the statements do not appear to concern. We just saw this at work in discussing Lewis's analytic effort. In effect, Lewis assumed that the analysis of these notions had to parallel the structure of the standard semantics (more or less). In other words, it had to conform to the central tenet. Then he delivered half the goods by telling us what the worlds were supposed to be like, but he didn't really complete the package by establishing the relevance of these other worlds. Unwary buyers bit on the terminology.

Metaphysics becomes more central when Kripke extends modal propositional logic by adding first-order quantifiers, and for a subtle reason. It is not that the extended semantics makes metaphysical assumptions that weren't made in the propositional case. Rather, it is that *controversial metaphysical matters affect the actual scope of the semantics.* Kripke, in effect, attempted to delineate a class of quantificational model structures by means of a complicated definite description, but it is not obvious exactly what entities satisfy that description. The semantics itself takes no stand on the crucial metaphysical questions. Put somewhat differently, what Kripke put forward may be taken in incompatible ways by philosophers of different metaphysical persuasions.

Here is why. The first step toward interpreting sentences with quantifiers is the enrichment of the notion of a model structure by the addition of a function, Ψ, which maps each member of K to a set of individuals. For any H in K, Ψ(H) is the 'domain' over which quantifiers are taken to range in the assignment of truth values to formulas with respect to H. Extending the 'possible-worlds' gloss, Kripke suggests that we regard Ψ(H) as the set of individuals that exist *in the world H*. But of course the 'worlds' really remain indices, with their internal natures irrelevant, so that what Ψ really does is just to *associate* a set of individuals with each member of K. The 'in' is not literal, for H might be a giraffe and you might yet belong to Ψ(H).

The missing metaphysics is now before our eyes. The scope of the semantics depends on what 'individuals' are included in the domains Ψ(H). If you are a commonsensical *actualist* (like me) then you will think something must actually exist in order to be a member of a set. As a result, you will think that no Ψ(H) includes unicorns or Sherlock Holmes. But if you're a Meinongian *possibilist* you will likely think lots of sets include individuals that don't actually exist, and that any such set is available to serve as a Ψ(H) in a quantificational model structure.[10] Surprisingly (to me anyway), in some of his intuitive remarks, Kripke himself sounded like a possibilist, for example in suggesting that Sherlock Holmes might be a member of some Ψ(H).[11]

Also surprisingly, although the semantics is literally neutral on this question, it tilts very strongly toward possibilism

---

[10] Lewis is a special case. Though not a Meinongian, he admits sets that include 'merely possible' objects, but these objects enjoy full-blooded existence. The indexicality of 'actual' restricts it to proper subsets of what exists, and the sets float serenely detached from the worlds and hence from considerations of actuality.

[11] In considering whether to give a truth value, with respect to H, to an open monadic atomic formula, for an assignment to its variable that is not a member of Ψ(H), he says 'Holmes does not exist, but in other states of affairs, he would have existed' (Linsky (1971: 65)). (Much later, in the Addenda to *Naming and Necessity*, he retracted the remark. See Kripke (1972, 1980: 158).) See Marcus (1993), essay 13, for a valuable discussion of merely possible objects in the context of Kripke's semantics.

precisely because it mimics the central tenet of world theory—the notion of possibility as truth in some possible world. If we accept this tenet and also think that it's possible that Sherlock Holmes exists,[12] then that possibility can only be secured *straightforwardly* in the semantics by invoking a model structure including a Ψ(H) with Holmes as a member. So an actualist would have to depart significantly from the straightforward application of the semantics in order to capture such a possibility. As a result a committed actualist has a substantial *prior* philosophical reason for doubting the adequacy of possible worlds semantics and would perhaps do better to seek a different analysis of the notion of possibility (which of course is the main goal of this book).

Despite this, philosophers of all metaphysical persuasions, including actualists, have tended to follow the modal logicians in presuming that an analysis of modal notions would have to conform to the fundamental tenet, and so they have not hesitated to postulate possible worlds. As I think of it, they have bitten an ersatz silver bullet. They have assumed that a certain strictly *mathematical* device—among any number of alternatives—and one that was originally enlisted for service in a formal semantics for a certain formal logic, *must* play the central role in our ultimate understanding of the *intuitive* notions of possibility and necessity.

There is irony here. For the philosophers' worlds are anything but mere indices, and there is no general agreement as to their ultimate natures. But on any account they are stunningly complex, 'maximal' entities of one or another ontological sort. And in sharp contrast with the logicians' worlds, the internal natures of these worlds are conceived as providing the underpinnings of the intuitive modal notions. Burdened by the central tenet, this *is* the only plausible way to proceed,

---

[12] In fact I don't (and neither does Kripke (1972, 1980: 158)), but that topic will be taken up later.

for the logicians have not told us, so to speak, how possibility gets going. In any given model structure it is just laid down in advance which predicates are satisfied by which entities in each world H, and then the inductive semantical machinery takes over and generates the truth values of the formulas across all the worlds. So, in effect, all of the work was already done in selecting K and providing the extensions of the predicates with respect to each member of K.

So if we feel we *must* avail ourselves of possible-worlds semantics in trying to analyze or illuminate the notion of, say, metaphysical possibility, then we can only get started if we are prepared to delineate a specific quantificational model structure. We can get started only if we're already there. This is not a defect of modal logic for it is, after all, only logic, and we really shouldn't expect logic to settle controversial philosophical issues. There are no silver bullets in logic. So the philosophers, in filling out possible worlds, are in turn only doing what they should be doing given that they've accepted the central tenet. They are, in effect, delimiting the choice of a model structure by telling us what the worlds themselves are like. The only problem here is the blithe acceptance of the central tenet—the assumption that we cannot get to the bottom of the intuitive modal notions without invoking other possible worlds.[13]

But really, if something is possible, for example your having been a politician instead of a philosopher, then of course that is a truth right here in the actual world. It's a fact about how *you*, and to that extent *this very world*, might have been. Intuitively, it has nothing to do with how other people (and other worlds) happen to be. (In this respect it differs from relational properties like

---

[13] A notable exception here is Chihara (1998). Chihara proposes an approach to modality that conforms to the central tenet while remaining nominalistic about possible worlds. Another interesting and literally worlds-free idea is Tony Roy's (1995) notion of a 'partial story' (or a partial world) where maximality is dropped but the basic quantificational approach to modality is retained.

being married or being a sister.) So I think it should be seen as a counterintuitive leap to presume that such everyday modal facts consist in facts about *other worlds*. I believe the conformity of standard modal semantics to the central tenet has tended to blind us to its counterintuitive nature. It really ought to seem very odd to think that any actual-world truth that doesn't obviously concern 'other worlds' should either *be* a fact about other worlds or else *depend on* facts about other worlds. If there are any other worlds, after all, then the signal fact about them is that they are *not* the actual world.

I think typical modal truths are just facts about our world, and generally facts about very small parts of it, not facts about some infinitude of complex, 'maximal' entities. At the very least, if there's a plausible way of understanding modal facts without going beyond what is actual, then it ought to be preferred to any account that makes them depend on (or be identical with) other-worldly matters. Thus I will later strive to analyze the modal concepts in a way that appeals only to what actually exists.

These recent considerations reflect a deep and fundamental weirdness that I believe must attach to *any* proposed possible-worlds analysis of modality. I think this weirdness has so far managed to escape our notice because we've fallen under the spell of possible-worlds talk (and our general reverence for technical logic doubtless played a role in our susceptibility to the spell). But when the weirdness is recognized, we are able to see that something very basic has gone wrong.

The weirdness is this. Suppose it's necessary that all **A**s are **B**s. The central-tenet *analysis* is that in every possible world, all **A**s are **B**s. So the necessity arises from what goes on in all the worlds taken together. There's nothing intrinsic to any **A**-containing world, even in all of its maximal glory, that *forces* all of its **A**s to be **B**s. It's as if it just *happens* in each such world that all of its **A**s are **B**s, that from the strictly internal point of view of any world, it's *contingent*, a mere coincidence. But then shouldn't we expect that this internal contingency will not be repeated in every world, that there will be worlds where some **A**s 'happen' not to be **B**s? After all, nothing within any given world prevents it, and these are supposed to be *all* the possible worlds.

The fundamental problem is that in world theory, what passes for necessity is in effect just a bunch of parallel 'contingencies'. The theory provides no basis for understanding why these contingencies repeat unremittingly across the board (while others do not). As a result, it provides no genuine analysis of necessity. What looks superficially like an analysis is really just the flip side of the central tenet: *Of course* if something is necessary, *and* there really are all these 'possible worlds', then the something that is necessary will be true in each of them. But that doesn't tell us *why* it is true in each of them, in other words, what its necessity consists in. A world theory that held such necessities to be intrinsic to its worlds would have the central-tenet biconditional as a consequence but not as an analysis. Either necessity would be taken as primitive or else the intrinsic features grounding the necessities would provide the analysis. In neither case would there be any evident need for nonactual worlds.

If you ask a possible-worlds theorist whether there are any worlds in which horses aren't animals, you will be told that there are not. (Here I assume horses really are animals.) And if you ask how we know this, the answer will be that the necessity of horses' being animals is intuitively clear. I think this response is correct and that it should immediately raise the suspicion *that the necessity doesn't arise from how the worlds are, but rather: that the worlds are taken to be as they are in order to capture the intuitive necessity*.[14] Yes, it does seem intuitively clear that horses are

---

[14] Here I agree with Kripke, who explicitly denies that 'possible worlds' figure in the 'ultimate nature' of modality, and claims that 'judgments involving directly expressed modal locutions certainly come earlier', asserting that the idea of a

animals of necessity, but now exactly what is the source of this clear intuition? Is it reflection about infinitely many complex, maximal entities, or is it reflection about the properties of *being a horse* and *being an animal*? A possible-worlds analysis seems to require intuitive insight into the former since the necessity is supposed to consist in—to emphasize, just *be*—this fact about all possible worlds. We would somehow have to intuit the pattern of locally accidental instantiation of those properties throughout all possible worlds. Just thinking about the properties themselves could not do the trick.

But in fact it's *precisely* what does the trick. We try to imagine a horse that isn't an animal and we fail. In other words, we try to imagine something instantiating *being a horse* but not instantiating *being an animal*, and we fail. Surely this isn't about infinitely many complex, maximal entities, but rather just about the two properties. *I find it a stunning irony that it's on the basis of this very spare thought experiment, not involving 'possible worlds' at all, that people so readily declare that there's no possible world in which a horse is not an animal.* The worlds, to the extent that speaking of worlds might be reasonable, merely reflect our thoughts about the properties. I claim these thoughts are thoughts about the real source of possibility and necessity. The possible worlds of logicians and philosophers are, respectively and at best, convenient mathematical and metaphorical devices. The former device distributes truth values to modal sentences the way the logician wants them distributed. The latter, however elaborated, captures the philosopher's intuitions about relations among various properties. But if we really want to *analyze* possibility and necessity, we will have to look past the veil of possible worlds to the real source of these modal notions.

possible world 'comes at a much greater, and subsequent, level of abstraction' (1972, 1980: 19, fn. 18). That subsequent level of abstraction is a certain *mathematization* of the intuitive concepts, and according to the present thinking, it is not one that provides a genuine analysis.

Worlds in General

Thus I hope that for the remainder of this book you will set aside any preconceptions you may have about how modality should be analyzed, including especially the powerful prejudice that any analysis must somehow involve special entities called possible worlds, whether of Lewis's variety or any other. For I'm going to point toward a very different analysis, one that I find immensely more plausible metaphysically. In a certain very general way it's similar to Lewis's proposed analysis, for each has its own special ontology, but the items of my ontology have a built-in 'modal character'—the needed oomph. Both analyses also rely on further properties or relations. Lewis's ontology was the infinitude of detached concrete realms, and the further properties and relations were the property of *truth* and an uncertain number of *counterpart* relations, but we failed to find the needed oomph in either the 'worlds' or the 'counterpart' relations.

In contrast, I believe there's just *one* world, which I don't mind calling the actual world. But I don't believe it's entirely concrete, and I have no opinion as to whether the concrete part is spread out in a continuous single spacetime, or fragmented into who knows how many detached and mutually inaccessible parts. But, as you already know, I don't think these unknown circumstances have any bearing on the analysis of modality, so I think our ignorance here doesn't matter.

I think modality has to do with relations involving the *abstract* part of the world, specifically with relations among (Platonic) properties. It is here that we will find the needed modal oomph.[15] Although I don't think it's ultimately essential, this view of modality is most easily described if we posit an *abundant*

---

[15] Ted Sider has suggested that this might be called a 'governance' view, and in a certain way this is entirely apt. It is a view according to which modal facts about the concrete part of the world are 'governed' by relations that hold in the abstract part.

realm of properties. Many philosophers, going back at least to Plato, have exploited properties for a wide variety of important philosophical objectives quite apart from coping with modality. So I think it's a dramatic understatement to say that Platonic properties have broader and deeper antecedent philosophical credibility than do modally enhanced detached concrete realms. As putative entities whose existence we can't verify in any remotely direct way, properties are overwhelmingly more plausible.

3. Abstract Worlds[16]

At the outset of this chapter I speculated that Lewis's account of possible worlds is probably not accepted by most philosophers today. Instead, those who have any ontological view at all about worlds typically see them, in one way or another, as certain abstract entities. As noted earlier, efforts to find suitable abstract entities to view as worlds generally take the intuitive modal notions as primitive, with the consequence that one would not then be able to invoke them in company with the central tenet to provide an analysis. One might wonder then why so many elaborate efforts have been made in this direction. One possibility, perhaps the best, is that philosophers in the grip of the fundamental tenet thought that the tenet would be made more credible if it could be demonstrated that the idea of possible worlds was at least *coherent*, and one way of doing this would be to show, with no analytic commitment, that certain abstract entities could mimic the structural behavior that would be required of worlds for the tenet to work its presumed modal magic. At any rate, abstract worlds have been conceived in a variety of literally incompatible

---

[16] This section is somewhat technical and inessential to the overall work at hand. It may be viewed as an appendix to the present chapter.

but more or less interchangeable ways. For example, they have been conceived as certain *states of affairs*,[17] as certain *sets of propositions*[18] and, as we will consider here, as certain special *propositions*.

Here we consider what I see as the simplest of the various approaches. We give it with a series of definitions:

1. A proposition is *consistent* iff it is possible for it to be true.
2. A proposition P is *maximal* iff for every proposition Q, either P entails Q or P entails not-Q.
3. A (*possible*) *world* is a maximal consistent proposition.
4. A proposition P is *true at* a world W iff W entails P.[19]

It is clear that this approach depends on the concept of possibility (as well as on a modal notion of entailment). It is also clear that this notion of worlds can be useful only if there really are maximal consistent propositions.

But how do we know there are? It cannot follow from mere definitions. Moreover, we would need a comprehensive theory of propositions, properties, and relations—a veritable *Principia Mathematica*—to make a good case for the existence of such worlds. To my knowledge no single such theory enjoys the allegiance of a majority of proponents of these abstract entities. (This is in contrast with the case of set theory, where the Zermelo–Fraenkel axiomatization dominates.) But here I will try to show that any comprehensive theory with certain rather natural features would be unable to accommodate maximal consistent propositions.

So let us imagine that we have a comprehensive theory of properties, relations, and propositions. We will conceive of them as entities of their own special kinds, not as set-theoretical

---

[17] Plantinga (1974).   [18] Adams (1974).
[19] I am not sure who first proposed this specific treatment of abstract words, but I believe it is by now the standard approach. It is essentially the view that Lewis calls 'magical ersatzism'. He criticizes the view in Lewis (1986: section 3.4), but under the assumption that 'ersatz worlds' have no inner structure.

surrogates mimicking the structural roles of properties, relations, and propositions. I will try to show that in the context of such a theory, along with a few seemingly reasonable assumptions, the hypothesis that there exist maximal consistent propositions is untenable. The first assumption, very general, is that the theory reflects our ordinary thinking in allowing properties, relations, and propositions to be instances of properties, and further, that it admits propositions about properties, relations, and propositions. We now turn to a few more specific assumptions and definitions concerning these entities.

Definition 1: A property P is *subextensive to* a property Q if every instance of P is an instance of Q. We assume that for any property P there exists a property of being subextensive to P.

We assume further that *functions* are certain sorts of relations between properties and that the familiar notions of one-one function, onto function, domain and range of a function, and the like may be fully developed within the theory and without invoking sets. Thus we may write, for example, 'f: P $\to_1$ Q' to mean that f maps P one-one to Q. We now adapt Cantor's set-theoretic notion of relative size to the case of properties, with the instances of properties playing the role of the members of sets.

Definition 2: Let P and Q be properties with instances. Then P >> Q if there is some function f such that f : Q $\to_1$ P but there is no function g such that g : P $\to_1$ Q. Intuitively, P has more instances than Q.

A final assumption is that for any proposition P, there is a property of being entailed by P, which we will denote by 'E$_P$'. Following our earlier convention (from which we will ultimately depart) we represent 'x is an instance of y' by 'x μ y'.

Now we will prove an analogue of Cantor's Theorem by an analogue of the standard proof.

Cantorian Claim: Let P be any property and let P_S be the property of being subextensive to P. Then $P_S >> P$.

Proof: It is clear that there exists a function f: $P \rightarrow_1 P_S$. (e.g., let q μ P. Then define f(q) = the property of being q.) Now suppose, for *reductio*, that some g: $P_S \rightarrow_1 P$ and consider the property C that an arbitrary instance y of P has iff some x is such that x μ P_S and g(x) = y and not-(y μ x). (This is the property of being in the range of g (on P_S) but not an instance of its image under the inverse of g.) Clearly C is subextensive to P and hence g is defined on C. We now ask whether g(C) is an instance of C.

1. Suppose g(C) μ C. Then some instance x of P_S is such that g(x) = g(C) and not-(g(C) μ x). But that instance of P_S is C itself (since g is 1–1). So it follows that not-(g(C) μ C).
2. Now suppose not-(g(C) μ C). Then it is not the case that some instance x of P_S is such that g(x) = g(C) and not-(g(C) μ C). But there is an instance x of P_S such that g(x) = g(C), namely x = C. So it must not be that not-(g(C) μ C). So g(C) μ C.

Combining 1 and 2 we have g(C) μ C iff not-(g(C) μ C), a contradiction. (QED)

We now show that under the present assumptions (including those made in the proof of the claim) that there are no worlds in the present sense. Thus for *reductio* let W be a world and consider E_W, the property of being entailed by W. Then consider the property, S, of being subextensive to E_W. By the Cantorian Claim, $S >> E_W$. Since W is maximal, for each instance P of S, either W entails the proposition, P_1, *that some instance of P is true*, or else it entails the proposition, P_2, *that no instance of P is true*. But now let f be defined on S by f(P) = P_1 if W entails P_1, and f(P) = P_2 if W entails P_2. Since

W is consistent, f is a function. Obviously f: $S \to_1 E_W$. But this contradicts the fact that $S >> E_W$.[20]

These considerations do not in themselves show that the present concept of worlds is incoherent. What they show is that under certain assumptions it is incoherent. The defender of this conception of worlds may reject one or more of these assumptions in order to defend the conception. But it should by now be clear that such a maneuver will not stand on its own. It can only be maintained in company with a full-blown theory of properties, relations, and propositions, something that the defenders of like conceptions of abstract worlds have generally not provided.

It should also be clear from this discussion that providing such a theory is not a straightforward task. Properties and propositions are set-like entities in their apparently unlimited capacity for applying to properties and propositions. Propositions, in particular, seemingly have the sinister capacity of quantifying over propositions including themselves. This obviously raises the red flag of potential paradox. The upshot is that any full-blown theory would (like set theory) have to resort to more or less unnatural devices in order to retain the hope of consistency. We would have to see on a case by case basis whether a given theory with such built in devices would or would not make room for maximal consistent propositions. It is not obvious that any theory could avoid paradox and make the needed room while remaining reasonably full-blown.[21]

---

[20] Similar Cantorian criticisms of abstract worlds are made in Grim (1984) and Jubien (1988), but the 'worlds' in question involve sets. See also Chihara (1998: 120–41).

[21] I am grateful to Greg Ray, whose comments helped make this section both simpler and clearer.

4

THE CORE ANALYSIS

1. Speaking About Things

THE philosophical work of Carnap, Quine, Marcus, Kripke, and many others, amply illustrates that the topic of possibility and necessity is closely tied to the concept of reference. We cannot expect to develop a plausible analysis of modality without a simultaneous, if not prior, understanding of how our singular terms and quantifier expressions are connected to individual entities in the world. Nowadays it is often claimed, for example, that ordinary proper names 'refer directly' to individual things and that (typical) quantifier expressions 'range over' individual things. But it isn't really obvious how the word 'things' (or 'objects' or 'entities', etc.) should be understood in claims like these. Typically, it is simply taken for granted that we already understand these terms. But I think it's a major mistake to take it for granted, and that we have to resolve this somewhat delicate matter before we can arrive at a plausible analysis of the modal notions or a plausible theory of reference. Roughly speaking, the difficulty here is a consequence of the great divide. It proceeds from the empirical facts about our different ways of thinking about things that the great divide encapsulates: we are able to think about things merely as physical objects, but also as objects of familiar kinds, and much depends on which kind of thinking we are doing.

To illustrate, let's briefly consider the intuitive proposition that all horses are animals. The sentence 'All horses are animals' evidently expresses this proposition, but there are two different ways to think about how it achieves this. One is to take the phrase 'all horses' as somehow picking out (or ranging over) the world's *horses*, in one fell swoop. Then the predicate goes on to assert of the horses that they are animals. Seen this way, the phrase 'All horses' is what we might call a 'horse-quantifier' and the sentence is only 'about' horses, as an ordinary speaker would doubtless see it. So this sort of approach would reflect our intuitive understanding of the English. Although there might be different ways of developing it in detail, any would seem to require an abundance of distinct quantifiers, matching the abundance of categories into which things may fall.

The other way of taking the sentence is reflected in first-order logic, where in effect we take the phrase apart, understanding 'all' to range (in general) over lots of things in addition to horses, but then letting 'horses' restrict the application of the subsequent predicate to the things in the wider range that satisfy the condition of *being a horse*. The effect of this approach is to make the sentence assert that each and every *thing* (under consideration) has the ('conditional') property of being such that *if it's a horse, then it's an animal*. On this 'unitary' view of quantification, the sentence is just as much 'about' (say) *statues* as it is about *horses*. It's about each and every *thing* (in the relevant universe of discourse), irrespective of any familiar and narrower category into which it might fall. This way we operate with a single, category-neutral quantifier.

These two treatments pair naturally (though maybe not inevitably) with contrasting ways of thinking about and describing our physical surroundings. In parallel with the multiple-quantifier view, we may see physical reality as made up of *horses, statues, stars, puddles*, and so on. Of course each horse, etc., also has the property of *being a physical object*, but on this way of thinking its status as a horse is somehow 'more fundamental'. The picture that pairs with the single-quantifier view reverses this. We see physical reality as made up of what are 'fundamentally' just (*physical*) *things* or *objects*. Some of these things of course have the property of *being a horse*, others the property of *being a statue*, and so on.

But aren't the two pictures interchangeable? Contemporary philosophical writing about reference and ontology generally proceeds as if the answer is affirmative but without actually addressing the question. This is evident in the readiness of philosophers to 'translate' English, with its seeming multitude of kind-driven quantifiers, into first-order logic, with its single wide-open quantifier. This may be harmless, but then again it may not. So we really need to ask whether there is any real difference between viewing physical reality as consisting of horses, statues, etc., and viewing it as consisting of physical things with such properties as being a horse or being a statue. It is, after all, easy to see the latter as just a slightly wordier equivalent of the former and, properly understood, I think it is. But the fact is that we speak and reason differently about horses and statues than we do about the very physical objects—on the present view, the mereological sums of fundamental-object stages—that happen to be the horses and statues. That we do so (and how we do it) is the substance of the great divide.

Thus imagine that we're thinking of physical reality as composed 'fundamentally' of horses and statues, etc. (which, again, are of course physical entities). Now consider a statue. In this way of thinking, when we refer to or quantify over this entity, we are referring to or quantifying over *a statue*—in effect, we're using a statue-quantifier. I think this has a profound effect on which properties we're intuitively inclined to regard as *essential* to the entity, the most obvious being its status as a statue. Thus, merely for example, a possible-worlds enthusiast would very naturally be inclined to think that if we 'consider this entity in another world', we will automatically be considering a *statue* (in fact, *that* statue).

But now shift to the view of physical reality as composed 'fundamentally' of physical objects. On this view, when we refer to or quantify over this very same entity, we're referring to or quantifying over a *physical object*, one that merely *happens* to be a statue, but very easily might not have been, might have been a birdbath or a planter, or just a blob having no significant shape or artifactual status. It won't be seen as essential to the mere physical object that it's a statue. And the philosopher of possible worlds will think that if we 'consider this entity in other worlds' it will *not* automatically be a statue. In some worlds it will be a birdbath or a blob.

Given that the great divide is essentially correct and examples like the one just given are accepted, it will obviously be very risky to move in our modal thinking from claims that are, at the intuitive level, 'about the statue', to claims that are, again intuitively, just 'about the physical object'. It won't follow from our conviction that the statue is essentially a statue that the physical object is as well, for it is also our intuitive conviction that the physical object might not have been a statue. I suggested earlier that there's a clear and straightforward way to reconcile such seemingly incompatible claims, and to do so without resorting to the implausible view that they're about distinct entities. The idea was to avoid the 'object fixation' and bring reconciliation by understanding them not merely as claims about certain *entities*, but also as claims about certain (different) *properties*. This strategy will play a vital role in the general approach to modality taken here, and will be treated in more detail soon.

I hope it now seems clear that there are potential modal differences between taking our physical surroundings as consisting fundamentally of horses and statues (etc.) and taking it to consist fundamentally of physical objects (that happen to fall into familiar categories). In what follows I will adopt the latter picture, and with it the single-quantifier approach, thereby siding with first-order logic as opposed to intuitive

English. (So I am also siding with the typically unexamined approach of standard philosophical analysis, which seeks to illuminate the workings of natural and philosophical language by idealizing into first-order logic.) I do this for several related reasons. First, it is fully general, and thus fits neatly with convention Q and with the Platonic Principle of Constitution. To be a horse is just to be a physical entity that has a certain property. Moreover, this approach makes easy room for physical objects that fall into no familiar categories at all (and the alternative may not). Of course it achieves this without losing the horses, which again are to be found among the physical objects. Second, it is more 'naturalistic'—it doesn't award any special standing to categories that happen to be important to us (horses, statues). Third, it does not prejudge any interesting questions about how to analyze modal notions. (For instance, it is compatible with a possible-worlds approach.) Fourth, there is a very important sense in which *being a physical object* really ought to be our most fundamental category for dealing with physical reality. It's the only natural property that everything out there has. The other categories are all more restricted and so are best viewed as special cases of this fully general and fundamental category.

Thus I am going to aim for an analysis in which our (singular) physical-object quantifiers are taken to range over all physical objects (ultimately understood in accordance with convention QPO of Chapter 1), not just piecemeal and severally over those that happen to fall into familiar, narrower categories, and notably not under any requirement that for each physical object there be a unique, nontrivial, and restricted category (whether familiar or unfamiliar) into which it falls. This decision will not prevent us from speaking specifically of horses any more than adopting standard first-order logic would. I believe it will become clear that this strategy allows for the full recognition of the seemingly conflicting modal intuitions that flow directly from the great divide, and in fact facilitates their reconciliation.

88   *The Core Analysis*

In particular, it will not jeopardize those modal intuitions, for example about statues, that seemed to accompany the multiple-quantifier understanding of our talk about things. They will find their proper place in the overall picture. In order to carry out this strategy we will need at our disposal certain special sorts of properties and also a fundamental relation.

2. Entity-Essences

For any entity of any sort at all, abstract or concrete, I assume there is a property of *being that specific entity*. For want of a better term, I will call such properties *entity-essences*. I assume that entity-essences are *singulary* in the sense that they cannot be instantiated by more than one thing at a given time. Moreover, I assume that no entity-essence is such that it is, or might be, instantiated by something at a time, but might also have been instantiated by some other thing at that time. Let's call this the property of *modal exclusivity*. Not all singulary properties are modally exclusive. For example the property of *being president (of the United States)* is singulary but not modally exclusive. Entity-essences are also assumed to be *temporally exclusive* in the sense that they cannot be instantiated by a given thing at one time and by a different thing at another.[1] (The property of *being president* is not temporally exclusive.)

For most ordinary physical objects, I have already (in Chapter 1) proposed an account of what it is to be a specific such object, based on the fundamental-object stages of which it is composed and the spatiotemporal origins of the fundamental objects of which they are stages. But I also followed Quine in adopting convention Q, and according to Q (with or without P and O) there are yet more physical

---

[1] This, of course, is already a consequence of perdurantism.

objects. For example, there are point-sized parts of elementary particles, mereological sums of such point-objects, and the like. In each case the 'Q-object' in question involves parts of fundamental objects whose entity-essences have already been secured, and the fundamental-object/origin treatment of the more ordinary Q-objects was accordingly extended to these more exotic ones. I will call the entity-essence of a physical object an *object-essence*. It is obvious that object-essences are not *haecceities* as these properties have typically been conceived. Haecceities are supposed to be primitive and non-qualitative, and object-essences are neither. It should also be clear, as claimed earlier, that there are uninstantiated object-essences, and that there is nothing either exotic or mysterious about them. They are utterly natural properties that happen not to have instances.

I am also assuming, but without analysis, that abstract entities like properties have entity-essences. I believe that for any specific entity x, whether abstract or concrete, there must be a property of *being x*. I see this as a special case of the Principle of Constitution. Any property, say p, is a *specific* property. One of the 'ways that p is' is being the specific entity that it is. By the Principle, its being this way consists in its instantiating some property. The property in question is the entity-essence of p—the property of *being p*. It is singular and both modally and temporally exclusive. *Being p* is *not* the property of being identical with p. That property is *relational*, with the identity relation as an intuitive constituent. It is 'projected' from that relation by taking p as a parameter, so it cannot serve to give p its specificity since it presupposes it. The present treatment of modality will rely on the existence of entity-essences for properties, but without requiring that they be analyzed so as to complement the object-essences. We may think of them simply as primitive gifts of the Platonic ideology.

The Core Analysis

3. K-Essences

Entity-essences are special cases of a much more general notion. In the domain of the physical, this more general notion encompasses not only object-essences, but also *dog*-essences, *planet*-essences, and so on. For any kind k and entity x of kind k, x instantiates what I call a *k-essence* (with schematic 'k' intended to suggest 'kind'). So object-essences are simply k-essences where the kind k is *physical object*.

To illustrate the more general notion, imagine that you have a dog. Your dog, and of course any dog, is a *specific* dog. So there's a property of *being that specific dog*. This particular dog-essence is in fact instantiated by a specific physical object, which therefore of course also instantiates a certain *object*-essence. But the dog-essence and the object-essence are two different properties. The object-essence could only have been instantiated by the specific physical object that does instantiate it, that is, by that very physical matter. But the dog-essence, which is in effect just our concept of that specific dog, might easily have been instantiated by a different physical object, by different matter. It's uncontroversial that some of the stuff that is in fact incorporated into the present temporal slice of the dog's body might not have been; for example, if its nails had just been clipped. In this event, the object instantiating that very dog-essence would have instantiated a *different* object-essence, simply because it would have been a different physical object.[2] It is equally clear that the object that in fact does instantiate the dog-essence need not have. It need not have been a dog at all, much less that

---

[2] This makes the term 'k-essence' rather misleading, for in general a k-essence is not an intuitive 'essence' of a single thing. It's an 'essence' we would intuitively associate with, say, a single dog, but now we need to be mindful of the fact that different things could have had that same dog-essence. Greg Fitch and Ted Sider have criticized this terminology for this reason, but I haven't been able to think of an alternative that relieves the intuitive discomfort without being overly cumbersome. (It isn't that difficult to get used to it.)

dog. Like object-essences, arbitrary k-essences are singulary properties.

It is very important to realize that the singularity of k-essences is not a theoretical stipulation or hypothesis. Rather, it is merely the Platonic reflection of the fact that our everyday thinking about specific physical objects and specific objects of familiar kinds, like dogs, does not tolerate the possibility of more than one thing's being a certain specific object, or dog, etc. Imagine someone, while pointing first to one dog and then to another, saying 'Do you see that dog? Well, *that's* that dog too'. This bizarre conversational gambit would more likely be taken to be absurd than simply false. Our concepts of specific things, if they are to be represented Platonically in accordance with the Principle of Constitution, accordingly require representation by singular properties.[3]

Object-essences and arbitrary k-essences have a certain built-in modal character, reflecting the great divide in various ways. That an object-essence does not tolerate possible instantiation by different objects reflects the object/parts side of the divide, the side that motivates mereological essentialism. This is generally not the case with k-essences. Our concept of 'a certain dog' (or statue, etc.) tolerates a range of possible constitutional differences, as we just saw, and other differences as well. (Here we are on the familiar kind/parts side of the divide.) We ordinarily allow that at least somewhat different stuff might have constituted 'the same dog', and that 'the same dog' could have been smarter or better trained or born a little later or earlier, or in a different place, etc. As emphasized in discussing the divide, I think this is just a matter of empirical fact about how we actually think 'about specific dogs', etc. Exactly how much constitutional difference we tolerate when it comes to a certain dog (or statue, museum, etc.) is unclear, and I'll make no claim

---

[3] I'm grateful to Greg Fitch and David Copp for insisting that I address this point explicitly.

about it.[4] All that matters is the unquestionable fact that we do tolerate some. Any uncertainty about how much just reflects the vagueness of familiar general terms, and addressing that phenomenon is a different (and of course major) philosophical project. For present purposes, it's best if we idealize by pretending there's no vagueness. I think none of the principal conclusions of this book would be undermined by any specific account of or resolution of vagueness.

4. Property Entailment and the Core Analysis

Being square 'entails' (or 'involves') *having linear sides*; *being yellow* entails *being colored*; *being a spouse* entails *being married*; *being a horse* entails *being an animal*; and so on.

The idea of entailment as a relation between properties is not new. But I believe it has generally been misunderstood, even by philosophers who are entirely comfortable with Platonic properties. Philosophers typically offer a modal analysis of the notion, specifically: for P to *entail* Q is for the proposition that all P's are Q's to be necessary. Then they generally take *necessity* to be truth in all possible worlds (or else take it as primitive). As we shall see, I think this analysis is backwards, that the necessity rests on the entailment, not vice versa, and of course that 'possible worlds' play no role at all in the matter.

At this stage it may help to recall our basic Platonic principles. We are taking properties to be genuinely existing entities, and all entities of course stand in various relations to each other. We are also assuming that for something to be a horse *just is* for it to instantiate the property of *being a horse*, and similarly for being an animal. But this venerable Principle of Constitution would not really be plausible unless

---

[4] I will, however, say a little more about the important case of person-essences in Chapter 5.

the properties *themselves* were taken to differ from each other in their intrinsic natures (which of course are atemporal and immutable on this ancient view). Instantiating, say, *being a statue* constitutes a thing as being a way that is different from how something is constituted by instantiating, say, *being a horse*. This idea would be indefensible if those properties did not differ intrinsically, for the relation of instantiation does not differ between cases of instantiating the two properties. So from the Platonic perspective there's an utterly natural explanation of our intuitive feeling that any horse *must* be an animal. *It's that the two properties' intrinsic natures together guarantee it.* We may therefore see this connection as an 'intrinsic relation'—one that holds between the two properties strictly as a result of their individual intrinsic natures. Here is the locus of the needed 'modal oomph'. Differences between properties' own intrinsic properties establish modal connections between them.

This view of entailment does not depend on any specific doctrine of property constituency. The property of being a horse entails the property of not being a xylophone, but the latter property is surely not an intuitive constituent of the former (nor is the un-negated property). Being a horse and being a xylophone are nevertheless properties whose internal natures guarantee that anything that instantiates the former property also instantiates the negation of the latter.

So it is an ontological feature of this Platonic view that it's automatic that if and when something instantiates *being a horse*, it also instantiates *being an animal* (and *not being a xylophone*). *This* is why the proposition that all horses are animals would be true 'in each possible world'. It wouldn't 'just happen' in each world that all the horses were animals (the way it *would* just happen in a given world that all the horses were wild). Something about *being a horse* would make it so, whereas nothing about *being a horse* would make a wild horse wild. I call that something—that intrinsic relation—*entailment*. Thus

I hold that the necessity of the proposition consists in the entailment of the one property by the other (and of course that possible worlds of any variety are superfluous).

I have no opinion about the ultimate nature of property entailment (though in the past I've entertained mereological hypotheses). In fact I think the ultimate nature of entailment will not be discovered by philosophical reflection. What philosophy delivers is the conclusion that ordinary properties have complex intrinsic natures. It doesn't provide details, which are a legitimate matter for theoretical postulation, with various candidates conceivable, and with the usual sorts of extrinsic considerations available for evaluating competing theories. But for present purposes such details don't matter, so I will refrain from theorizing along these lines. Once it is given that certain entities have complex internal natures, a variety of intrinsic relations automatically hold between them. For practical purposes, we may as well think of the entailment relation as primitive (but with no commitment to simplicity). All we need for the further development is the authority of the conclusion that entailment does indeed hold or fail to hold between pairs of properties as a result of their intrinsic properties. This enables us to begin analyzing necessity and possibility. A substantial chunk of the analysis is already before us. For example, the necessity of the proposition that all horses are animals consists in the fact that the property of *being a horse* entails the property of *being an animal*.

Just as necessity of this '*de dicto*' variety rests on entailment, possibility rests on an intrinsic relation that is its natural partner, and which I call *compatibility*. The possibility of there being wild horses consists in the compatibility of the properties *being a horse* and *being wild*. Compatibility and entailment are 'dual' notions and so are easily interanalyzable: for example, for two properties to be compatible is for neither to entail the negation of the other.

5. Analysis and Reduction

Now is a good moment to pause and address an important question, one that arose earlier in connection with possible worlds. Is the present bit of analysis 'reductive'? Just what is a reductive analysis in the first place? As I see it, an analysis of a concept tells us what the concept *is* by telling us what its constituents are and how they are combined in the concept. So if the concept under analysis has a certain characteristic feature, say being a *mental* or a *mathematical* concept, then one would think that feature must also somehow be present in the analysans, or else the analysis could not be correct. If we take this seriously it can easily seem surprising that so many philosophers have so eagerly sought 'reductive' analyses. From this perspective it looks like the pursuit of magic. Despite this, philosophy abounds with what are typically taken to be clear cases of reductive analysis.[5]

Let's pause briefly to look at a common venue for supposedly reductive analyses: physicalist philosophy of mind. I will suggest that the supposedly clear cases are really no such thing. For the sake of a simple and familiar example, and not worrying too much about details, let's consider the type–type identity theory of the mind. On such a view, the ultimate analysis of the mental would consist of a collection of separate analyses of specific mental concepts like *being in pain*. Thus it might be held that the analysis of *being in pain* is: undergoing C-fiber stimulation. The stimulation of C-fibers is uncontroversially a *physical* phenomenon in the sense that it is (at least in principle) fully describable in the vocabulary of physics. Many have thought that if all mental concepts had analyses conforming to this sort of pattern, then *the mental*

---

[5] For example, see Sider (2003) for a defense of the effort to give 'a definition of the modal in terms of the non-modal' (184). Sider sees Lewis's proposed analysis as genuinely reductive in this sense.

would have been reduced to the physical. And many have made similar claims about more sophisticated physicalist approaches including token–token theories. But there are three different ways of taking such a claim of reduction.

(1) One would be as a claim that there really are no mental phenomena, and that our seeming to be subjects of mental phenomena yields to some purely physical explanation involving only physical phenomena like C-fiber stimulation. On this way of thinking the mental would have been reduced to the physical by having been *eliminated* in favor of the physical. (2) A second understanding would be that although there really are mental phenomena, there are physical phenomena that underlie them in a strictly covariant way, so that in the ultimate scientific study of the mind we may ignore the mental and focus on the physical. On this view the mental would have been reduced to the physical in the sense of the latter providing satisfactory surrogates for the study of the former. (3) A third understanding would be that mental phenomena are strictly *identical with* certain physical phenomena, so that far from being eliminated, they have merely been demystified. The mental would have been reduced to the physical in the sense of failing to have any nonphysical constituents.

The first understanding of the reduction claim is recognizable as the familiar doctrine of eliminativism. The second goes naturally with the view commonly known as property dualism but also accommodates epiphenomenalism. Whatever the merits of these positions might be, and granting that each would in *some* sense be 'reductive', neither is compatible with the idea that we have in hand a reductive *analysis*. We can see this easily at the level of the pain example. The *analytic* claim that *to be in pain* is *to undergo C-fiber stimulation* is a claim to the effect that a certain property has certain constituents arranged in a certain way. But the eliminativist is denying that there is such a property as the former in the first place (or at least denying that we often instantiate it), while happily accepting the existence (and frequent instantiation) of the latter. But this is flatly incompatible with the analytic claim. Similarly, while the property dualist (or epiphenomenalist) accepts the former property, he is insisting that it is not the same property as the latter, which property merely underlies it (or just accompanies it) in a certain way. But the analytic claim is that they are one and the same property.

Only the third conception is compatible with the analytic claim. I think of the third view as (*physicalist*) *inclusionism*: the mental is included in the physical. The claim is that mental phenomena are to be found among physical phenomena. Only inclusionism is compatible with a genuine physicalist *analysis* of mental concepts. But such analyses are *not* reductive because they do not analyze the mental by appealing to the nonmental. It is a consequence of the analysis, properly understood, that *undergoing C-fiber stimulation* is an often-instantiated *mental* property, for it *is* the property of *being in pain*, which is uncontroversially a mental property. So it seems to me that reductive *analyses* are hard to find even in the branch of philosophy perhaps most commonly thought to offer them.

It is often said, perhaps with more modest intent, that physicalist identity theories reduce mental *discourse* to physical *discourse*, with the latter regarded as nonmental. Such a view might be held by an inclusionist who concedes that the mental itself has not been reduced to the nonmental. There is indeed a sense in which it would be a linguistic reduction: paradigmatically mental discourse would be replaced by paradigmatically physical (and nonmental) discourse. (Thus talk of pain might be replaced by talk of C-fiber stimulation.) But here we must not overlook the fact that what underlies this very modest linguistic reduction is a purported analysis that is *not* reductive. 'Undergoing C-fiber stimulation' may indeed be a paradigmatically physical term, but if the identity analysis is correct then it happens to express a perfectly ordinary *mental* concept: *being*

98   *The Core Analysis*

in pain.[6] (A parallel comment applies to the paradigmatically mental term 'pain'.)

Let's return now to modality. *De dicto* necessity is generally thought to be a paradigmatic modal concept. If it is, and if the correct analysis of the necessity of all A's being B's is—let's just say schematically—that the property of *being (an) A bears relation R to the property of being (a) B*, then it seems to me that the relation R *must* be modal—even if we might not previously have thought so—for R would then be the source of this species of necessity. A broader moral, not required here but surely tempting, is that *any* concept has characteristic feature F if and only if, in a correct analysis of that concept, the analysans also has F. Of course one might become convinced of the correctness of an analysis and then conclude that the concept did not have the originally supposed feature F after all. Alternatively, one might conclude that what initially seemed a congery of non-F concepts was really imbued with F after all. It might go either way. What seems difficult to imagine is a correct analysis of a genuinely-F concept in entirely non-F terms.

Of course here I'm taking the schematic analyzing relation R to be entailment in the sense described above: a standing relation that holds immutably and intrinsically between certain pairs of properties. On this view it is the source of necessities like the one just considered and therefore it is a constituent of any parallel claim of *de dicto* necessity. So, to the extent that such necessities are modal, so must be this relation, even if one might initially have thought that standing intrinsic relations between Platonic properties are unlikely to have such a feature. So I am claiming no 'conceptual reduction' in offering the present

---

[6] I believe that when we speak of concepts as publicly available entities ('the concept of pain', 'the concept of C-fiber stimulation', etc.), as opposed to our individual subjective representations of such concepts, the nonsubjective concepts are simply properties and relations. See Jubien (1997: chapter 1) for more on this topic.

analysis. I don't think any successful analysis of these modal notions could provide such a reduction.

Now let's recall the earlier discussion of Lewis's proposed analysis, which is widely thought to be reductive in some important way. In Chapter 3 I argued that when we think of Lewis's 'worlds' merely as detached concrete realms, they have no relevance to nontrivial possibility, and the analysis, understood in these terms, would be implausible. We are now in a position to see that it would be implausible *precisely* because it would be 'reductive' *in the sense of purporting to analyze a modal concept with only nonmodal resources*. On the other hand, if we could somehow endow the 'worlds' with the kind of oomph required for modal relevance, then the result would cease to be reductive in this sense and, if the oomph were understood in the most natural and direct way, it would even threaten circularity.[7] Of course, there might be other ways of understanding it that were noncircular and even reductive in some more plausible sense.

For example, there is a *linguistic* sense in which Lewis's proposal—modal oomph aside—would be 'reductive' simply as a result of its structure, and this may help explain the widespread impression of *conceptual* reductiveness. Lewis often expresses it by saying the modal operators are quantifiers over worlds. For example he says this in discussing the box and diamond of modal logic. But then he also says, more generally, that '... possibility amounts to existential quantification over the worlds ...'; and '... modality turns into quantification ...'; and also 'Modality *de re* ... is quantification over possible individuals'.[8] Here he moves from claims about modal operators (or symbols like boxes and diamonds) to claims about modality itself. I suggest that what motivates all of this is the basic idea that certain perplexing *linguistic constructions*—prominently the

---

[7] Shalkowski (1994) and Chihara (1998: section 8.6) express similar worries.
[8] Lewis (1986: section 1.2).

modal adverbs—are *eliminable* in favor of simple quantification provided we admit certain sorts of entities into our ontology. So there would be a reduction of one sort of linguistic construction to another. But I still insist that this could be correct only if the concept expressed by the original construction were none other than the one expressed by the quantificational one. So it would not legitimately count as a conceptual reduction of a species of modality to something nonmodal.

Returning to the present analytic suggestion, it cannot be overemphasized that Platonic properties are supposed to have fixed intrinsic natures. How they are in themselves depends in no way on the concrete realm. *Being a horse* would be no different intrinsically if there had been no horses, no different if all horses had been wild, no different if some had been blue, and so on. Similarly for *being an animal*. That one property entails another is a matter of fact on all fours with the fact that one horse is taller than another. Of course the former is a fact about the Platonic realm while the latter is not. So, where modal propositions may once have seemed to transcend the *actual*, they now seem only to transcend the *concrete*. The boundaries of possibility and necessity are not determined by nonactual circumstances, but rather by actual relations among properties. That horses must be animals does not depend on there being no inanimate horses among 'nonactual entities', but rather simply on the entailment we've been discussing.

6. Essentialism and Modality *de re*

At this point I hope it seems plausible that the entailment and compatibility of properties offers a sound basis for analyzing *de dicto* modality. Now let's set our sights on modality *de re*. I believe entailment and compatibility, along with some of the special properties described above, are the only tools we need to extend the analysis. But I also believe modality *de re*

Essentialism and Modality de re

is not all it's cracked up to be. As the analysis unfolds I will urge that typical claims of nontrivial *de re* necessity are in fact false, and I'll also try to show that it's a fundamental error to identify the doctrine of essentialism with necessity *de re*. The error stems from the seductive lure of object fixation and thus from a failure to respect the great divide. I believe a closer look at essentialist thought experiments will yield a better understanding of the true nature of essentialism, and also that the thought experiments provide good reason for taking that doctrine seriously once we've seen what it is and what it isn't.

Quine argued that although we might be able to make some sense of the modal notions as applied to *sentences*, we can't make sense of modality as applied to *things*. A well-known example goes like this. Suppose we agree that it's necessary that cyclists are two-legged and mathematicians are rational. (Ignore the actual implausibility of these specific claims.) Now suppose we have on hand someone who is both a cyclist and a mathematician. If we *describe* this person merely as a cyclist, then he will necessarily be two-legged but he won't necessarily be rational. But the opposite holds if we describe him merely as a mathematician. Quine concluded that the attribution of an essential property to a thing made sense only with respect to a prior description of the thing—that the unqualified attribution of an essential property to a thing was nonsense.[9]

I think this is a very interesting argument. For one thing, ignoring Quine's extensionalism, it virtually concedes that genuine modality at least sometimes resides in relations between properties, for it is being taken that two-leggedness is a consequence of the description of the person as a cyclist. In effect, *being a cyclist* is being imagined to entail *being two-legged* (and *being a mathematician* to entail *being rational*). So the cyclist's being necessarily (or essentially) two-legged is taken to consist in this entailment, and of course I think this

[9] Quine (1960: 199).

conception is fundamentally correct (again with details of the actual example aside). But then there's a crucial mistake. For Quine assumes that to attribute (say) rationality to the *thing* independently of its being a cyclist or mathematician (etc.) would be to do something utterly different from attributing the property to it under some such description. Typical critics of the argument don't question this, but they do urge that the argument fails, insisting that the utterly different notion makes perfectly good intuitive sense after all.[10] I think everyone here is at least partly mistaken. The argument fails, but the notion is *not* utterly different. I believe the failure of the argument traces directly to the fact that the notion isn't (relevantly) different at all.

To be a specific physical thing, on the present account, is nothing more nor less than to instantiate a certain object-essence. Setting dualism aside, let's suppose x is the physical object that is our cycling mathematician. Just as *being a cyclist* entails certain properties and fails to entail certain others, so it is with the object-essence *being x*. For example, given mereological essentialism, if z is a part of x, then *being x* entails *having z as a part*. Of course, *being x* doesn't entail *being rational* or *being two-legged*. But this hardly shows that it *doesn't make sense* to assert that these properties are essential to x. To the contrary, it makes perfectly good sense, as the example of *having z as a part* reveals. The problem is just that it's *false* that the object x is essentially two-legged or essentially rational.

As I will analyze them, these claims are false precisely because these properties are *not* entailed by *being x*. I am therefore urging that the *de re* is a special case of the *de dicto* and hence needs no separate analysis of its own.[11] Roughly

---

[10] For example, see Kripke (1972, 1980: 39–42). He uses different examples to make the point.

[11] This is not a novel suggestion. For example, Plantinga (1974) offers a 'special case' treatment. The details are rather different, reflecting a different understanding of the nature and role of proper names.

speaking, we have a case of modality *de re* when (and only when) the appropriate property in the *de dicto* formulation is an *object*-essence. Because object-essences (and entity-essences generally) are singular and could not be instantiated by different entities in different circumstances, it is they that do the '*res*' work in modality *de re*.

We may illustrate this by considering a well-known Kripkean thought experiment. Suppose a certain physical object w instantiates a certain table-essence, the property of *being such and such table*, and that w is in fact made of wood. The *de re* claim, of w, that *it* is necessarily (or essentially) made of wood (suppressing the existential presupposition) is the claim that the object-essence, *being w*, entails *being made of wood*. But notice that this entailment is precisely the truth-condition for the classic *de dicto* formulation, *necessarily, for any x, if x instantiates being w, then x instantiates being made of wood*, as proposed in the core analysis given in Section 4.4. In contrast, to say that the *table* is necessarily made of wood is to say that the table-essence, *being this table*, entails *being made of wood*. This, of course, is just the analysis of the *de dicto* claim that it's necessary that anything that instantiates *being this table* also instantiates *being made of wood*. Moreover, it isn't a *de re* claim because different objects could have instantiated the table-essence. Intuitively, *it is a claim about a specific table, but without being a claim about a specific object*. It is object fixation that leads people to take 'This table is necessarily made of wood' as a case of modality *de re*.

Returning to the *de re* claim, *being w* does not entail *being made of wood* since the parts of w might have been arranged so that it wasn't made of wood. So it isn't necessary that anything that instantiates *being w* also instantiates *being made of wood*. But if the familiar Kripkean thought experiment is right, and we couldn't have *this table* without its being made of wood, then the table-essence, *being this table* indeed does entail *being made of wood.*[12] Hence, to infer with Kripke that the *object* w is essentially made of wood, from the intuited premise that the *table* is essentially made of wood is mistaken. On the present analysis, it would be to infer that *being w* entails *being made of wood* from the premise that *being this table* entails *being made of wood* (given that w instantiates *being this table*).

I believe that a careful consideration of the entire gamut of Kripke's essentialist thought experiments reveals that while they indeed offer support for conclusions of the latter sort, they offer none at all for the former. In fact, I think that Kripke drew the proper conclusions from the experiments, but then fell into erroneous *de re* claims by what he took to be innocent paraphrase.[13] What seemed to be innocent was anything but, and it was a textbook case of object fixation. As a very important consequence, I believe it's a serious mistake to follow Kripke in thinking of essentialism as the doctrine of nontrivial *de re* necessity.

7. Essentialist Thought Experiments

Earlier I urged that our thoughts about relations among properties are the real source of our intuitions about necessity and possibility. I believe this claim is well supported by a careful consideration of Kripke's essentialist thought experiments. Now is a good time to explore this further.

It's a commonplace among essentialists that *being a person* is essential to each of us. A series of Kripkean thought experiments that favor this conclusion might run along the following

---

[12] Actually, the claim is more plausible if we take the property to be being originally made of wood.

[13] Notice how, in Kripke (1972, 1980: 47), he moves from 'this table' to 'this very object' without missing a beat in pressing an essentialist claim: '*This table* is composed of molecules. Might it not have been composed of molecules? ... it's hard to imagine under what circumstances you would have *this very object* and find that it is not composed of molecules'. [My emphasis.]

Essentialist Thought Experiments

lines. First we ask, say, whether we can imagine 'having Nixon without having a person'. Now, just what do we do in trying to imagine this? Suppose we first imagine a yacht. Perhaps we say to ourselves, 'Well, that's not Nixon'. Then maybe a palm tree, with the same conclusion. An alligator? A zombie? No. Perhaps we next conjure up a visual image of an entity that looks a lot like Nixon. Maybe a life-size cardboard Nixon-prop, or an automaton. Well, again, we haven't imagined Nixon. Finally we imagine someone who looks and acts a lot like Nixon, and gives no sign of being otherwise. Then we may conclude we've somehow imagined Nixon, and yes, in doing so we've imagined a person. The net effect of these extensive imaginative efforts may be that we feel Kripke is right: we can't imagine Nixon failing to be a person.

But exactly why are we entitled to the initial negative conclusions? For example, when we imagine a palm tree, what is it that guarantees we haven't imagined Nixon? I think there is only one plausible answer: At some level, we know that *being a palm tree* is incompatible with *being Nixon*, and the imagining simply helps make this vivid. The same holds for the yacht, zombie, and so forth, and would hold for any sort of thing that isn't a person. It's important to see that it would be ludicrous to think that our imaginings somehow ensured that the palm tree (etc.) wasn't the *physical object*, say x, which actually happens to instantiate *being Nixon*. Here we have no way of thinking about x in isolation from the fact that it happens to instantiate the property of *being Nixon*.

Finally, why are we entitled to conclude that in the last part of our thinking, we actually did 'imagine Nixon'? Say we formed a visual image of a man wearing a dark suit, with a certain sort of hairline and a forced smile, about to enter a helicopter, arms raised so as to form a 'V', etc. Certainly nothing about the visual image *itself* made it an image of Nixon. This very image would have worked perfectly well if we had been asked to imagine an actor in a movie doing a scene depicting Nixon's final departure from the White House. And it is just as clear that there was nothing in the image itself that made it an image of the physical object x. It can only be that conjuring up the image counted as imagining Nixon—given that it did!—because part of the conjuring was the *intention* that it represent Nixon. (Certainly not the intention that it represent x.) The property of *being Nixon* is therefore intimately involved in our being able to imagine Nixon. We cannot give our imaginings the right representational force unless this property plays a role in our intentions.

With this in mind, let's return for a moment to the palm tree. What is to prevent someone from imbuing an image of a palm tree with the intention that it represent Nixon, or better, that it represent something as instantiating *being Nixon*? One might imagine Nixon's body being disassembled down to its atoms, or even further, and then reassembled as a palm tree. A likely reaction would be that this is not to represent a palm tree as Nixon *because Nixon is a person and therefore not a palm tree*. Nixon went out of existence at some point in the disassembly and never took a second bow. What this evidently reveals is that most people *already* think being a person and being a palm tree are *incompatible*, and so are unable to apply the right sort of Nixon intention to the image. Another possibility might be trying to imagine Nixon having the *form* of a palm tree, yet still being a person. We might imagine, for example, that what was superficially a tree-like entity had an internal structure complex enough to support sophisticated thought. But then most people would say it wouldn't really be a palm tree if it had such a complex internal structure. This again seems to presuppose that being a person and being a palm tree are incompatible. It therefore seems that success in imaging Nixon as a palm tree would require a conception of these properties that rendered them compatible. Surely any such conception would be far from typical.

The fact is that we don't typically view what seem to be palm trees as though they might be sources of human-like thought. If we're reluctant to cut down a certain palm, it won't be because we're worried that it might be a thinking being. Thus I believe the incompatibility of these properties is built into our ordinary thoughts about them and the things that have them. Essentialist thought experiments, to the extent that they succeed, rely entirely on such features of everyday thought.

As a result I believe the thought experiments are best understood merely as picturesque reflections on entailments and compatibilities of properties that are already deeply embedded in our thinking and our linguistic behavior. Moreover, they are (generally) *not* thought experiments about specific physical objects. They help make it clear that *being Nixon* entails *being a person*, is incompatible with *being a palm tree* and so forth. There is nothing at all in these experiments to warrant any similar conclusions about the physical entity x. (As far as the experiments go, *being x* may very well be compatible with *being a palm tree*, and it certainly doesn't entail *being a person*.)

8. Canonical Examples

It may be useful to set out clear examples of the present analytic proposals using the language of quantified modal logic. There is some danger in doing this, because it might suggest that I think there is a uniform way to represent ordinary English formally. Certainly there is a tendency in contemporary philosophy to present formal systems in the effort to capture the philosophical essence of one or another fragment of natural language, but I have no intention of doing that in this book. In fact, as we will see later, I don't think the modal aspect of our language would yield to a uniform formal approach. I think we are more likely to arrive at a genuine understanding of modal talk on a case-by-case basis and that it's better *not* to seek a comprehensive formal systematization. For an easy example, I very much doubt that ordinary speakers make a natural and ready distinction between typical sentences that lead off with a modal adverb and those that place it in the 'scope' of a quantifier. Ordinary language is simply not regimented so precisely that it may be adequately captured by smooth translation into a formal idiom with its inevitable built-in regimentation.[14] With these caveats in mind, we proceed to look through the lens of logic at the differences among three standard sorts of cases.

De dicto Cases

(1) Necessarily, all horses are animals.

It may be that sentences like this are sometimes uttered with something other than what we may think of as *de dicto* intent. We won't worry about that. We will proceed as if (1) were synonymous with '(The proposition) that all horses are animals is necessary' (or '... necessarily true'). In the familiar language of modal logic, and making instantiation explicit, we may represent such a sentence by

$$(1^*) \quad \Box \forall x(Ixh \to Ixa),$$

where 'I' expresses the instantiation relation, 'h' denotes the property of *being a horse*, and 'a' denotes the property of *being an animal*.[15] We may take 'h' and 'a' to be directly referential

---

[14] This is even clear without modality. For instance it is common for people to utter sentences of the form 'All **A**'s are not **B**'s' in order to express the intuitive proposition that not all **A**'s are **B**'s.

[15] Here I depart from the earlier informal 'aRb' style of notation (with 'μ' for instantiation) in order to conform more closely to typical formal versions of the language of quantified modal logic.

singular terms. According to the present analysis, for it to be necessary that all horses are animals is simply for (the property of) *being a horse* to entail (the property of) *being an animal*.

(2) Possibly, some horses are blue. (Or: It's possible that some horses are blue.)[16]

Again, let's assume a context requiring the intuitive *de dicto* reading. The formal representative would then be

$$(2^*)\ \Diamond \exists x(Ixh\ \&\ Ixb),$$

with 'b' referring directly to the property of *being blue*. Our analysis is that the possibility of there being blue horses consists in the compatibility of the properties *being a horse* and *being blue*.

De re Cases

(3) All (physical) objects are necessarily spatiotemporal. (Each physical object is such that it is necessarily spatiotemporal.)

This is a genuine case of modality *de re*. It explicitly concerns *objects*. The standard translation into the language of modal logic, again equipped with explicit instantiation, would be something like

$$(3^*)\ \forall x(Ixp \rightarrow \Box Ixs),$$

---

[16] It's worth noticing that, perhaps in contrast with (1), the most natural reading of (2) is probably epistemic. This is of course not the reading I'm pursuing here. It isn't that easy to find a truly natural English sentence that seems to compel the formalization to be given. One candidate is: 'There might have been blue horses'. (2) is awkward English at best. It reflects the pretense that the modal adverbs of English behave like the modal operators of logic. That we philosophers are often presented with such sentences and do not balk at 'hearing them' along the lines of (2*) suggests that we have by now so internalized the formal logic that it has begun to shape our philosophical language rather than the reverse.

where 'p' denotes *being a physical object*, and 's' denotes *being spatiotemporal*. On the present analysis, the truth-condition of any formula of the form '□Ixy', for any assignment of an object o to the variable 'x', and property q to 'y', is the entailment of q by the object-essence of o.

(4) Any (physical) object is possibly somewhere else. (Any object might have been somewhere else.)

Here is another truly awkward sentence that only a philosopher would utter, and only under the influence of a desire that it be rendered formally by something relevantly like

(4*) $\forall x(Ixp \rightarrow \Diamond Ixe)$,

where, for simplicity of expression, 'e' denotes *being somewhere else*. A formula '◊Ixy', with object o assigned to 'x' and property q assigned to 'y' will be true, in accordance with the modal analysis, iff the object essence of o is compatible with q. (Note that on our treatment of object-essences, sentence (4) expresses a false proposition. It is, however, intuitively true that any object of our everyday acquaintance might have been somewhere else.)

Essentialist Cases

I argued above that the thought experiments favor a conception of essentialism that departs from necessity *de re* but nevertheless deserves to be called essentialism. On this view the following sentence expresses an essentialist claim, but without being a case of necessity *de re*.

(5) Any human is necessarily human.

In the recent tradition of modal metaphysics, it would go unquestioned that (5), using our present conventions, should be 'translated' by '∀x(Ixh → □Ixh)', which is straightforwardly *de re*. The thought experiments that would tend to back an assertion of (5) proceed, as detailed above, by asking us to try to imagine a *specific human* (like Nixon) failing to be human. We are supposed to fail in this imaginative effort, and to conclude that *that human* could not have failed to be human. Generalizing from the arbitrary choice of a specific human, it follows that no specific human could have failed to be human. From this, it is erroneously inferred—by object fixation—that some *entities* are essentially human. I believe the only misstep in this chain is the final, object-fixated inference. So I believe the thought experiments support (5), but not under the *de re* construal. I want to offer what I will call a (*genuine*) *essentialist* construal, one that reflects the gambit of the thought experiment in which we are asked to try to imagine a *specific* human not being human. The idea is to generalize on the *human-essences* of the various specific humans, rather than generalizing on the *entities* that happen to instantiate those human-essences. Thus, if we want a formal representative of the essentialist reading of (5) we need a piece of formal machinery that will enable this.

So we might introduce a function symbol, say '*' into the modal language that will have the effect of mapping an arbitrary kind k to the property of *being a k-essence*. The essentialist reading of (5) then would be something like

(5*) ∀x(Ixh* → □∀y(Iyx → Iyh)).

In logician's English, 'For any x, if x is a human-essence, then it is necessary that for any entity y, if y instantiates x, then y is human'. The present analysis then renders (5*) true iff every human-essence entails *being human*. Thus we are understanding (5) itself, under the essentialist reading, as saying that every human-essence entails being human. Notice that we are at liberty to regard this claim as restricted to instantiated human-essences or to take it more generally, as we wish. The logic-induced understanding would of course be the former, and we could build this explicitly into (5*) by conjoining '∃zIzx' to 'Ixh*' in the antecedent.

5

PROPER NAMES

So far I've tried to avoid the topic of proper names and examples that rely on them. But no discussion of modal notions is complete without taking up the topic of their interplay with names, and I begin that business in the present chapter. I think existing theories of names are unsatisfactory and my goal is to offer an alternative. I'm concerned here with theories of *ordinary* proper names—terms that would typically be regarded as names by ordinary speakers. Such names include names of existing people, places, animals, geological and astronomical entities, and artifacts like ships and buildings. Thus 'George W. Bush', 'Florida', and 'Mount Everest' are names in the present sense. But so are 'The Empire State Building', 'The Hope Diamond', and 'The United Kingdom' which, though they sound like definite descriptions, function in actual practice no differently than do the first three. (In some of these cases it is even clear that if the name were taken as a description, nothing would satisfy it. 'The United Kingdom' is a good example.) There are also ordinary names that presumably lack bearers—so-called 'empty' names—which usually have their origins in fiction, legend, tradition, or myth. These include 'Sherlock Holmes', 'Zeus', 'Atlantis', and 'The Fountain of Youth'. Some ordinary names are believed to be empty by some speakers, but not by others ('God', 'seven'). My procedure in this chapter will be to focus on names that unquestionably have bearers, saving empty names for Chapter 6.

In *Naming and Necessity*, Saul Kripke presented forceful criticisms of straightforward 'definite description' theories of names, including 'cluster' theories. Most participants in the subsequent discussion have found these well-known criticisms to be persuasive, and I won't recapitulate them. Partly as a result of Kripke's efforts, the so-called *direct reference* account of names has become the dominant view. But not everyone accepts it, and those who don't typically favor one or another 'sophisticated description' theory, in which name-backing descriptions are artfully chosen so as to evade Kripkean criticisms. In the first section of this chapter I will say briefly why I think neither of these approaches is plausible. Then I will begin to present the new theory.

Thus let's agree with Kripke that description theories of the sorts he dismissed in *Naming and Necessity* are incorrect and turn our attention to the direct reference and sophisticated description views. I believe each of these has serious problems that are avoided by the theory to be given here.

1. Contemporary Theories

(1) *Direct reference (DR) theories* are nowadays normally characterized against a backdrop of *propositions* (though Kripke himself was leery of 'the apparatus of "propositions"'[1]). For example, Jeffrey King writes that '... it is widely held that proper names ... contribute the individuals they designate ... to the propositions expressed ... by the sentences in which they occur. Such expressions [as proper names—MJ] are generally called *devices of direct reference*, the term "direct" alluding to the fact that these expressions don't contribute some entity to a

---

[1] Kripke (1972, 1980: 21).

proposition that ... determines an individual distinct from the entity. Rather, the individual itself gets contributed to the proposition.'[2]

From this perspective, a sentence like 'Bellamy Road was favored to win the 2005 Kentucky Derby' expresses a proposition that has a certain specific entity—one that is in fact a horse—as a constituent. In David Kaplan's vivid phrase, that entity is 'loaded into' the proposition by the name 'Bellamy Road' itself (but not quite the way the horse was loaded into the starting gate). In particular, the entity doesn't get into the proposition as a result of satisfying a definite description that gives the *meaning* of its name, nor as a result of uniquely possessing a property that its name *expresses*. In effect, *it is the entity itself that is the meaning*, though it isn't essential to accept this gloss. One might prefer to say that the name *has no meaning, only a referent* (or *bearer*). (We will return later to this ambiguity.) With this intuitive understanding of DR in place (while noting that a DR theorist is not automatically committed to any specific theory of propositions) we may ask whether DR captures the way ordinary proper names are actually used by competent speakers. I believe it does not. I'll now give two cases to motivate this and then draw some general conclusions.

Case 1: an artifact. Suppose you are a sculptor. You have a studio and you periodically receive shipments of clay. The clay is delivered in tubs. For a long time you have been doing preparatory work on what you hope will be your *magnum opus*, a clay statue of Daffy Duck with the name 'Daffy'. You have made countless drawings to help decide on the exact effect you want to achieve in clay. You've agonized over how antic Daffy's

---

[2] King (2007: 6–7). King mentions another and weaker sense of 'direct reference' (2007: 7n), but the weaker notion also relies on propositions. Soon I will mention an even weaker notion that is not dependent on propositions.

posture should be, how zany his expression, how ruffled his feathers, and the like. (Note that you and your friends easily use the name 'Daffy' during the period when the statue does not yet exist.) Finally you have it all firmly in mind and nicely sketched out. It's time to sculpt.

So you enter your studio and find three tubs of clay, each containing more than enough for the Daffy project. You say to yourself, 'Which clay should I use to make Daffy?' and carefully inspect the contents of the three tubs. Upon noticing that there are no significant differences in color or texture, you answer yourself aloud: 'It doesn't matter'. I believe that this judgment is absolutely correct. *Daffy* can be made from the clay in *any* of the tubs, and only someone in the grip of a philosophical theory would be inclined to dispute this. So you pick a tub and get to work. Much later Daffy is complete (and perhaps also an esthetic triumph). In thinking over the history of the project you reminisce about that first day in your studio and take wry pleasure in thinking *that Daffy might have been made of entirely different matter*. I believe this thought is entirely correct, and that no ordinary person would deny it. Again, it takes a metaphysical theory to engender any doubt about this.

Saul Kripke's principle of the essentiality of material origins is just such a theory.[3] Kripke arrives at this principle (though without exactly propounding it) by doing what we just did: by considering our ordinary intuitive reactions to specific cases. But the cases he considers do not have comparable detail and (partly as a result) *do*, as he carefully says, *suggest* the principle in question. But, to put it mildly, the present case suggests that the principle is incorrect. If we are to erect a theory on the foundation of our considered intuitions about cases, then we should strive to find one that accounts for as many as possible, and we should not let a tentative theory trump an incompatible intuition unless there seems nowhere else to turn.

---

[3] See Kripke (1972, 1980), especially pp. 113–14 and footnotes 56 and 57.

So now let's assume it's true that Daffy might have been made of entirely different matter. How does this fit with a DR theory of names? I think not well at all. If DR were correct, then 'Daffy' would load the bearer of the name—evidently a certain physical object—into propositions expressed by sentences using the name. Now, on the present metaphysical view, any physical object is just some specific matter, and any specific matter is just a specific mereological sum of stages of fundamental objects. One would think that this is a perfectly innocent and naturalistic picture, one that begs no interesting questions about reference and hence one that could easily be accepted by proponents of any naturalistic theory of reference. Moreover, DR theorists have generally not offered any different picture in pressing their view. But look where it leads.

The physical object that is the bearer of the name 'Daffy' would be loaded into the proposition expressed by 'Daffy might have been made of entirely different matter'. But then it would follow that some specific matter might have been made of entirely different matter. It doesn't take the influence of a philosophical theory to bring us to reject this outcome. So what is needed is a theory of names according to which such a sentence can be true, but *without* having the absurd consequence that some specific matter might have been made of entirely different matter. The theory to be offered here will satisfy this desideratum.

It's important to see that the conclusion that Daffy might have been made of different matter doesn't depend on Daffy's having a *name* (or on having had one before actually existing). What it depends on are the special intentional details of the case. Comparable details are not to be found in Kripke's cases. But in fact we can readily embellish even Kripke's familiar *wooden table* example so as to reach a Daffy-like conclusion. Suppose a prestigious woodworker wins a competition for a commission to produce a *very important* table, say for the royal palace. So he has already made careful drawings, perhaps a scaled-down model, etc., for submission to the distinguished panel of judges. Upon winning, he carefully examines the wood available from many different sources, and concludes that for each component part of the table there are several entirely acceptable pieces of wood. So the ultimate table, which we may assume has no *name*, might have been made of entirely different matter. Such intentional details are not normally present in the assembly-line production of run-of-the-mill tables like those we find in academic lecture halls, and it is in *these* cases that we are inclined to see the actual matter as essential to the table. But in less usual cases, cases with the imagined sort of surrounding context, the intuitive conclusion is just the one we have drawn. Somewhat loosely, we may say that the 'essential identity' of a given artifact—in this case a *table-essence*—may arise from different sources, and that sometimes the material origin is crucial and other times it is not.

Case 2: a natural object. We have it on good scientific authority that some of our planets were formed by the compaction of massive clouds of dust. Let's assume this is right, and consider the planet Venus and the specific dust from which it was formed. Surely Venus might have been formed from (at least) somewhat different dust. Intuitively, it simply isn't of the essence of Venus that it was formed of precisely the dust from which it was actually formed. At least *some* of its formative dust might have been too far away to have been affected by the compacting forces, and dust that was actually too far away might not have been.

The name 'Venus' of course does not correctly apply to the formative cloud, that is, the scattered mereological sum. It correctly applies to the entity that is the compaction of that cloud. That's the bearer of the name.[4] Intuitively, this compaction is,

---

[4] For simplicity, both here and later, I'm ignoring the subtleties of three- and four-dimensionalist theories of objects and simply speaking in our everyday way,

more or less, just a certain dramatic rearrangement of the matter that comprised the cloud. But no ordinary speaker would think that the matter comprising the formative cloud could have been *some other* matter, even some other largely overlapping matter (which might have become Venus). The very idea verges on—or even achieves—incoherence. To be completely clear, this is not to say that the *cloud* could not have consisted of somewhat different matter, for indeed it could; it is only to say that that very matter could not have been (somewhat) different matter. But, again, Venus is just a rearrangement of the matter of its formative cloud. So we must ask, how could it be that some specific matter, if arranged one way, *could* have been different matter, but if arranged a different way, *could not*? Intuitively, a given parcel of matter either just plain could or else just plain could not have consisted of somewhat different matter. We can't have it both ways.

To help solidify this, imagine a general (and modal) case of arrangement and rearrangement: First we have some matter arranged so that it could not have been (somewhat) different matter. Now rearrange it so that it *could* have been different matter. Of course we still have the very same matter. Now, in accordance with the supposed modal character of the new arrangement, imagine a situation in which that matter *is* different matter, and then a further development in which *that* matter is rearranged so as to have the original arrangement. It evidently now follows that the original matter, as originally arranged, could have been somewhat different matter after all and, moreover, in the very same arrangement.

So which will it be? Given some arbitrary matter, should we think that it just plain could have consisted of (somewhat) different matter, or should we think that it just plain could

---

in which planets and statues, etc., are taken to be three-dimensional objects that endure through time. We've already seen that I don't favor the elaboration of this everyday thinking into a metaphysical theory, but that is a different matter.

not? We have two very strong intuitions that now *appear* to conflict. The first is the pure intuition (about *matter*) that *no* matter (notably not the matter of the formative cloud of Venus) could have been different matter. This intuition reflects the object/parts side of the great divide, which is a driving force behind mereological essentialism. The second is the equally strong but not-so-pure intuition (about *Venus*) that Venus could have consisted of different matter. Here we are on the familiar-kind/parts side of the divide. Now consider the intuitively true sentence, 'Venus could have been made of (somewhat) different matter'. On the DR theory of names, 'Venus' loads a specific object—some specific matter—into the proposition expressed by this sentence. If this proposition is indeed true, as we normally think, it follows that some specific matter could have been different matter. Hence DR is committed to this incoherent possibility, and so to the rejection of the pure intuition. It is for this reason that I reject DR.

I believe that both the pure and the not-so-pure intuitions are correct and the new theory of names will accommodate them. (In fact I also think that Venus, like Daffy, could have consisted of *entirely* different matter, but I won't press this. A hint is that its *orbit* plays a matter-trumping identifying role akin to the *planning* in the Daffy and very-important-table cases.)

In Chapter 4 we discussed the difference between thinking of the physical world as consisting fundamentally of an array in spacetime of objects of familiar and not-so-familiar kinds, and thinking of it instead as consisting simply of physical objects, which often happen to be of familiar kinds. These seemingly divergent ways of thinking were linked to the great divide and were held to bear heavily on our understanding of reference and quantification, and on our intuitive estimates of essentiality. I chose to follow the physical-objects/single-quantifier approach and claimed that following it would not jeopardize the essentiality intuitions associated with the familiar-kinds/multiple-quantifier alternative.

Here it seems evident that this choice is driving the present objection to DR theories. For I am insisting that the bearer of the name 'Daffy' is a *physical object*. While I believe that typical DR theorists would agree at the outset that the bearer is a physical object, I also believe they have not noticed the present sort of difficulty. A typical theorist, under the influence of object fixation, would initially think that loading Daffy—a *statue*—into a proposition was nothing more nor less than loading a certain *physical object* into the proposition. But the present difficulty might lead such a theorist to think anew and seize upon the idea that although it's a *statue* that gets loaded in, it is somehow not just a physical object. This might be thought to provide a way to avoid the great-divide problem of the *object's* not being a statue essentially, since one would think that the *statue*—whatever exactly it is—is surely essentially a *statue*.

Thus a DR theorist might seek a different way of understanding the proposition *that Daffy might have been made of different matter*, one that avoids the absurd conclusion that I claimed derails DR. But the options are not inviting. They would be views according to which a *statue*—the loaded entity—(1) is not a physical object at all, (2) is only partly physical[5], or (3) is a physical object of a kind somehow different from a simple mereological sum of stages of fundamental objects.

It is very hard to see how such a view might be persuasively elaborated and defended. If it construed the bearer of 'Daffy'

---

[5] For example, it might be held that the statue is the mereological sum of the physical object and the property of being a statue (or the property of being *that* statue). Bealer (2004: 592–3) mentions 'qua-objects' as a possible option, but finds it a desperate refuge for a DR theorist: 'On this view ... *x*-qua-*F* is much like the ordinary object *x* except that the property *F*, which is not an essential property of *x* simpliciter, is an essential property of *x*-qua-*F*.' (592). In this important article Bealer offers a criticism of DR that does not rely on a Daffy/Venus-style strategy.

to be a nonphysical or only partly physical entity, then it would have to contrive for the intuitively true sentence, 'Daffy is a physical object' to be officially true, or else produce powerful reasons for us to abandon this intuition along with countless similar ones. On the other hand, if it took the bearer to be a physical object of a sort that could have such a property as being a statue essentially, it would owe us a clear metaphysical understanding of such objects, and would also seem committed to the counterintuitive consequence of there being more than one physical object in exactly the same spatiotemporal location. So it seems to me that the DR theory is simply not plausible as it stands, and that the sorts of metaphysical and semantical arrangements needed for its rehabilitation would be far from straightforward.

Now let's return briefly to the ambiguity in DR that was noticed above. It is possible to separate the question of what 'determines' the referent of a use of a name from the question of what meaning (if any) that token (or the name itself) possesses. Although it is sometimes assumed that if names have meanings, then it is their meanings that determine their referents, I do not assume this and the reason is that I think there are different notions of determination in the mix. Suppose someone uses a name on an occasion and we agree that the token produced 'has a referent' (or bearer). If, in asking what 'determines' the referent, we are asking what, in the natural history of the language, brings it about that the token has that referent, then I believe Kripke's 'causal chain' view provides the most plausible answer. But 'determines' might be intended in a weaker sense, so that the question would merely ask for (nontrivial) necessary and sufficient conditions for the token to have that referent. I will soon hold that names have meanings *and* that these meanings are properties that their bearers uniquely possess. So the fact that the use of the name expressed such a property would also 'determine' the referent in this weaker sense.

On the view to be developed here, the link between the name and its bearer is forged by the name-giver (if any) at the introduction of the name. This is of course the first link in the Kripkean causal chain. But we will soon see that the name-giver does not give the name its meaning even though it may be said to have its meaning from the start. Thus if we are considering 'determination' in the natural-history sense, the causal chain is what determines the referent. (In the weaker sense, again, both the causal chain and the meaning determine the referent.) There is a sense in which such causal-chain determination of referents is a 'direct reference' view simply because it doesn't pin the determination of the referent on any meaning the name might have (especially if the meaning is later held to be the bearer itself). In this weak special sense the present theory will be a 'direct reference' view, but the fact remains that the term is normally reserved for theories that either hold that names have bearers but no meanings, or else hold that the meanings are the bearers themselves. Both of these are of course views I do not accept. I should add that, as I use the terms 'bearer' and 'referent', the present theory will *not* be one on which sentences containing names are 'about' their bearers or referents in the most straightforward possible way, for that of course is the way of direct reference with loading-in.[6]

(2) *Sophisticated description (SD) theories.* Most efforts to find more sophisticated descriptions depend for their plausibility on the claim that the new descriptions are 'rigid designators' of the bearers of names. The reason, roughly stated, is that most theorists have accepted Kripke's claim that ordinary names are rigid designators, and they are seeking descriptions that will plausibly give the meanings of names and not merely fix their referents. This has led most SD theories to rely at some point on the idea that a definite description that is satisfied by

---

[6] I thank Marija Jankovic for a conversation that led to improvements in the last two paragraphs and for other helpful comments.

an entity only *accidentally* may be converted into one that is satisfied *essentially* by exploiting the concept of *actuality*. Thus consider the description 'the winner of the 2005 Kentucky Derby'. This description is in fact satisfied by a particular horse, but of course only accidentally. Some other horse might have satisfied it (even one that doesn't actually exist). So the idea is to 'rigidify' the description by inserting 'actual'—thus: 'the *actual* winner of the 2005 Kentucky Derby'.

There is a *key principle* behind this strategy, namely that such a 'rigidified' description, if satisfied at all, is satisfied *essentially*. Thus whereas *winning* is merely a contingent property of a certain horse, *actually winning* is supposed to be a necessary property. As a result, SD theorists sought to back proper names with rigidified descriptions in an effort to avoid the problems of earlier theories that stemmed from the merely contingent satisfaction of typical descriptions. (The rigidification strategy is often applied to descriptions that, ironically, exploit Kripke's own 'historical chain' suggestion about how the referent of an occurrence of a name is determined.)

But I think the key principle underlying the strategy is incorrect. I don't think the term 'actual' contributes any semantic content at all to the meaning of 'the actual winner'. I make the same claim for 'actually' in the phrase 'the horse that actually won' (and also for similar uses of 'in fact' and the like). In general, I believe these terms merely contribute *emphasis*. I think ordinary speakers of the language would not hesitate to say that some other horse *might have been the actual winner* or *might actually have won*.[7] Ordinary speakers would regard such statements as *obviously* true. Only speakers (such as most of us) who have internalized a standard 'possible worlds' conception of modality would have any difficulty saying these things.

---

[7] Notice that although a sentence like 'Bellamy Road might actually have won' is appropriate in two different sorts of contexts—those in which it is known that he didn't win and those in which it is unknown whether he won—it is nevertheless unambiguous. It means that he might have won.

Let's have a go at this from a slightly different angle. Suppose we allow ourselves the (actually, fairly common) phrase, 'in the actual world', and agree that it's more or less interchangeable with 'actually'. Now consider the (true) sentence, 'In the actual world, Giacomo won'. How tempted are you to think this sentence expresses a *necessary* truth? If you are, I suggest that the temptation is directly traceable to a disposition to think that there are possible worlds *in addition to* the actual world, and that true sentences of the form 'In the actual world, ...' are *necessary* because they're true in *all* possible worlds—this because you also think 'the actual world' rigidly picks out one and only one world. But if instead you think, as I do, that there is only one world, then there should be no temptation at all to think this sentence expresses anything other than the evidently contingent proposition that Giacomo won.

If this diagnosis is correct, then a person who thinks the sentence 'In the actual world, Giacomo won' is necessarily true, or who thinks that *being the actual winner* is essential to Giacomo, thinks such things as a result of accepting a *theory* with a certain kind of *ontology*. But when ordinary speakers use phrases like 'in the actual world' and even 'in the best of all possible worlds', they do so without commitment to any theory involving worlds. If George Steinbrenner (the owner of Bellamy Road) said, 'In the best of all possible worlds, Bellamy Road wins the Triple Crown', no one would have inferred that he believed in (or was committed to) the existence of possible worlds other than the actual world. He would have said this independently of any relevant ontological theory. He would merely have chosen a colorful way of saying that it would be best (at least from his point of view) if Bellamy Road won the Triple Crown, and he wouldn't have hesitated to accept this as a paraphrase.

Genuine possibilities, of course, are possibilities *for the world*. As detailed in Chapter 3, it seems to me that if something is *possible*, then that is a fact *internal* to the world. For example, I think the fact that Bellamy Road might have won the Derby is simply a fact about (a very small part of) the world, and specifically *not* a fact about *nonactual* worlds. As we saw, the ultimate analysis of such claims does not rely on the existence of other possible worlds. Hence I believe that SD theories fail because they depend on an implausible ontology of an implausible theory of modality. It is only through the lens of such a metaphysical theory that such theorists can see the relevant descriptions as appropriately 'rigidified', and in doing so they flout the language as it is *actually* spoken.

Further, and I believe more important, is that even if we accept the entire package incorporating the ontology of possible worlds, the rigid status of 'the actual world', and the claim that rigidified descriptions are rigid designators, we wind up with unintended and counterintuitive modal results. The reasons are embedded in the Daffy/Venus-type cases discussed above. Intuitively, Daffy is essentially a statue. Now suppose some rigidified description picks out the very *object* that bears the name 'Daffy'. Also intuitively, *that* object need not have been a statue. It might have been an undistinguished blob of clay (or a grossly scattered object, a different statue etc.) Now consider a world where the object is a blob of clay. If the rigidified description really is rigid, then it picks out this object in that world. The unwanted and counterintuitive consequence is that since the rigidified description is supposed to give the meaning of 'Daffy', the sentence 'Daffy might have been an amorphous blob' (etc.) turns out to be *true*. Thus we contradict our original intuition about the essential statuehood of Daffy.

So far I have said little about Kripke's famous term, 'rigid designator'. The term is usually explained against the backdrop of an intuitive understanding of possible worlds, but this isn't essential. Kripke himself has sometimes explained it by saying (roughly) that a rigid designator is a term that designates the same object when it occurs in modal (and other intensional) contexts as it does when it occurs in nonmodal contexts. It should be clear from what has already been said that both DR and SD theorists hold that ordinary names are 'rigid designators'. It is also clear that if the Daffy and Venus cases are accepted, then ordinary proper names simply are *not* rigid designators.

Something that isn't very clear is that DR and SD theorists really mean the same thing in claiming rigid designation or, more cautiously, that their claims have the same ramifications. For the DR theorist is thinking, intuitively anyway, that some specific object is loaded into the expressed proposition regardless of the nature of the containing sentence (again, even if no conforming proposition theory is officially accepted), while the SD theorist is thinking merely that some specific object satisfies a rigidified description associated with the name. If an SD theorist is operating with a standard treatment of definite descriptions (such as Russell's), then names do not load *any* specific entities into the intuitive propositions expressed by sentences containing them.[8] They are 'general' existential propositions (while the DR theorist's propositions are thought to be 'singular'). Intuitively, such a proposition is not 'about' the bearer of the name. What is in fact the bearer of the name is what just happens to make the sentence true if it satisfies the matrix. The fact that the description is rigid doesn't change this. But on the DR account, the sentence *is* 'about' the bearer of the name because the bearer is packed into the very proposition. Here the DR theories perhaps better reflect our intuitive understanding of the unanalyzed English, in which we surely take such sentences to be 'about' the bearers of the names. The present theory of names will feature 'aboutness', but without 'loading-in'.

---

[8] Recall that Russell—of course using his own terminology—is explicit about this in 'On Denoting'. See Russell (1905: 51).

2. Revisiting Intuitions and the Great Divide

Let's return to the pure and not-so-pure intuitions in Daffy/Venus-type cases. I believe there is a simple and uniform explanation for these intuitions, and it is nothing other than the great divide. Let's remind ourselves how this is supposed to work in these cases.

Turning to Venus, and thinking 'naturalistically', that planet is just a certain physical object—a hunk of matter—that happens to have many interesting properties, like orbiting the sun. According to the divide, when we think of this entity *merely as a physical object*, and specifically not *as Venus* or *as a planet*, etc., it seems to us that its parts are extremely important, in fact *essential*, to its being the very physical object it is. The reason is that a physical object is just an aggregation of matter, and we do not think that some specific matter could have been *different* matter (even in part). On the other hand, we happily agree that *Venus* (or *that planet*, etc.) could have consisted of at least somewhat different matter. So we don't normally think the actual parts of *Venus* are essential to it.

There is an intuitive reversal when we consider the *arrangement* of a thing's parts. When we think of what is in fact Venus merely as a specific *physical object*, the arrangement of its parts is insignificant to its identity. They could be arranged so that it was a widely scattered object, or as two separated hemispheres, or just permuted while remaining spherical, and so forth. It would still be the same matter, and hence the same physical entity. But as soon as we think of this object as a *planet*, or as *Venus*, the arrangement of its parts assumes great importance. Scatter them widely and we no longer have a planet, much less *Venus*. This is perhaps even more vivid with *statues*. If the clay constituting Daffy were reshaped into a sphere or a cube, Daffy would no longer exist. But of course the brute physical object would still exist. In our thinking, Venus and Daffy will both tolerate *some* (actual or modal) rearrangement of parts, but not arbitrary rearrangement.

As detailed earlier, the amount and type of rearrangement tolerated by an object of a familiar kind depends heavily on what specific *kind* is governing our thinking about it. Thus, for example, thought of as *a piece of clay*, the object that is Daffy will tolerate much more rearrangement than it will when thought of as *a statue*. (Roughly, it takes visible scattering to destroy its status as a piece of clay, but intact rearrangement, as we have seen, can easily destroy its status as a statue. In sharp contrast, at least for those of us who accept convention Q, no amount of rearranging destroys its status as a physical object.)

Suppose it is agreed, as I have repeatedly urged, that our ordinary thinking features this divide. Does it follow that in our everyday thought and speech we are systematically and overtly illogical? It may seem that it does. Let's resolve (naturalistically) that only as a last resort will we embrace the dark and counterintuitive view that more than one physical entity may occupy exactly the same spatiotemporal location.[9] Then what is evidently a single entity is at once a *physical object*, a *piece of clay*, a *statue*, and undoubtedly also an object of further familiar kinds. According to the great divide, the modal status of this entity with respect to parts and arrangement varies across all of these categories. Thus: (1) the physical object could have been widely scattered, but the piece of clay and the statue could not; (2) the physical object and the piece of clay could have been spherical, but the statue could not; (3) the physical object could not have been made of somewhat different matter, but the piece of clay and the statue could. And so forth.

---

[9] I find it surprising that some philosophers accept 'coincident objects'. The notion clearly offends against commonsense 'naturalism' about the world, so that it should be viewed as a last resort. Certainly it would not appeal to anyone aware of the great divide in ordinary thought and speech and alert to the dangers of object fixation.

I claimed that there is a very simple way of understanding the great divide according to which these varying modal intuitions are actually compatible. Although it is simple we have so far failed to see it. This is partly because it is heavily obscured by the usual ways of capturing such claims in the language of *logic*. So, in this instance, I believe our most powerful technical tool for achieving philosophical clarity has been applied with pretty much the opposite effect.

To be more specific, let's consider how the following sentences of English would typically be rendered in the language of quantified modal logic.

(1) The piece of clay could have been flat.
(2) The statue could not have been flat.
(3) The statue is the piece of clay.

First, we would let a predicate letter, say 'P' express the property of being a certain piece of clay (for example, a piece of clay on the table), and similarly for 'S' and the property of being a certain statue and for 'F' and the property of being flat. Then we would treat the definite descriptions in the manner of Russell:

(1*) $\exists x(Px \ \& \ \forall y(Py \to x = y) \ \& \ \Diamond Fx)$.
(2*) $\exists x(Sx \ \& \ \forall y(Sy \to x = y) \ \& \ \sim\Diamond Fx)$.
(3*) $\exists x \exists y(Sx \ \& \ \forall y(Sy \to x = y) \ \& \ Py \ \& \ \forall z(Pz \to y = z) \ \& \ x = y)$.

Clearly (1*)–(3*) are an inconsistent trio. So, to the extent that we feel that they capture the logic of claims (1)–(3), we will also feel that at least one of these claims must be rejected. But my suggestion was that these claims are not inconsistent. The central idea is that they are as much about *properties* as they are about physical objects, and that by taking this seriously we may reconcile them. In Chapter 1, I sketched the idea informally without packaging it in the language of formal logic. Although

I don't find it essential, some may be more comfortable with the idea if it is presented more formally, and there will in fact be a certain bonus in doing so. With the analytic tools of Chapter 4 in hand, we are in a position to proceed.

A first thing to notice is that the machinery of k-essences enables us to treat definite descriptions in a unified but non-Russellian way.[10] We are taking (1)–(3) to be about a particular piece of clay (e.g., the one on the table) and a particular statue. According to the present view, there is a corresponding piece-of-clay-essence and also a corresponding statue-essence. These properties are *already* singular, so utilizing them enables us to avoid an analogue of the Russellian uniqueness clause. Now let 'c' and 's' be directly referential names of the piece-of-clay-essence and the statue-essence. We will also let 'f' denote the property of being flat and use 'I' to express the instantiation relation. We may now translate (1)–(3) into the language of modal logic as follows:

(1**) $\exists x(Ixc\ \&\ \Diamond \exists y(Iyc\ \&\ Iyf))$;

(2**) $\exists x(Ixs\ \&\ \sim\Diamond \exists y(Iys\ \&\ Iyf))$; and

(3**) $\exists x \exists y(Ixc\ \&\ Iys\ \&\ x = y)$.

We may even take this a healthy step further by deploying the analysis of possibility *within* the formal logic so as to eliminate the diamonds. Letting 'C' express the *compatibility* relation, (1**) and (2**) become

(1***) $\exists x(Ixc\ \&\ Ccf)$; and

(2***) $\exists x(Ixs\ \&\ \sim Csf)$.

(Since there are no modal operators in (3**), it stands as it is.)

The bonus of this detour into formalism is that the object fixation of (1*) and (2*) becomes vivid. In the modal clauses

---

[10] Delia Graff Fara has developed a non-Russellian treatment of descriptions as predicates. See Fara (2001).

the respective properties make no appearance whatever. The modal part of the claim is strictly and solely about *objects*, because only an object could satisfy '◊Fx' or its negation. But in the new treatment, whether in double- or triple-star versions, the k-essences are carrying the modal weight. The new versions make it obvious why I claimed that the present theory features 'aboutness' but without 'loading-in'. The k-essences provide the aboutness. *They* are of course loaded into the proposition but the *object* that satisfies the matrix is *not*. Only a treatment like this can do full justice to (1) and (2) and the intuitions they capture.

Something like this effect might be achieved within the more typical framework by modifying, say, (1*) to

(1#)   ∃x[Px & ∀y(Py → x = y) & ◊(Px & Fx)].

This neatly brings the relevant property into modal play, but it does so at too high an intuitive price. The reason is that we have agreed that (at least somewhat) different objects might have been the piece of clay, the statue, and so forth. This revised treatment would thus remain object fixated by failing to accommodate this intuitive possibility.

3. Categories and Social Determination

I believe that, strictly as a matter of empirical fact, the vast majority of ordinary proper names have fixed *categories*. By this I mean that nearly every ordinary name has associated with it a certain property, which I call the *category* of the name, and if the bearer of the name ceases to have that property, then the name no longer correctly applies to it. Thus when Daffy is flattened or reshaped into a sphere or cube, the name no longer applies. The sculptor might say, 'Well, Daffy is now much better behaved', but we should recognize this as a tongue-in-cheek use, not a literal and correct application of the name. Daffy, in fact, no longer exists, for Daffy was a certain *statue* and even if we are encouraged to view the sphere or cube as a statue, it isn't the same statue—it simply isn't Daffy. Of course there is nothing to prevent the sculptor from deciding to *call* the reshaped object 'Daffy'. But this would be a case of applying a new and lexically indistinguishable name to the object,[11] even if the sculptor never consciously decided to call it by that name, and even if he confusedly thought he was using a name that the thing already had. Surely, if he decided to call it, say, 'Cube', no one would think that the object now had *two* names, or that it had been renamed.

For another example, imagine that the famous real estate investor Donald Trump buys a classic Bordeaux château, say (perish the thought) Château Margaux. Trump has it disassembled, has the parts shipped to Atlantic City and then has them reassembled into an art deco style casino. He might decide to call the result 'Château Margaux' but, intuitively, it doesn't *automatically* have that name, and if Trump makes this decision, then the intuitive judgment should be that he has introduced a new and lexically indistinguishable name, not that he has simply continued to call the object by a name it already has. After all, he might have decided to call it 'Château Trumpaux', and no one would have thought this was a renaming (or that the newly assembled building now had two names).

Or suppose that a Caribbean golf adventure goes wildly awry for Mr Trump when he looks for his ball in the deep rough, encounters foul play and is transformed into a (philosophical) zombie. Is it literally correct to say that Trump is now a zombie? Or is it correct to say that Trump no longer exists and that his body has become that of an entity that isn't a human being? Assuming that nothing could be a person without

---

[11] In fact to a *different* object under perdurantism. But in this section, for simplicity, we will for the most part work from the everyday, naïve endurantist perspective.

having some sort of mental life, the latter is the intuitively correct answer despite the fact that we are unable in practice to discriminate between people and philosophical zombies. That we would continue to apply the name merely reflects our epistemic limitations. (At some later point it might be appropriate to think we had a new, lexically indistinguishable name with a new category.)

A further, double-edged example will play an important role in guiding our thoughts about categories. Let's ask ourselves what the *New York Times* would report if Venus were: (1) blown to smithereens by a powerful explosion; or (2) dragged out of orbit by a tiny rogue black hole. I believe the answers are clear. In case (1) the report would be that Venus had been destroyed by an explosion.[12] In case (2) it would be that Venus was no longer a planet, and that it was drifting off to parts unknown in the galaxy. (There would no doubt soon be a website for sky buffs: perhaps 'trackingvenus.org'.)

I believe these examples reveal that our understanding of names involves what I will call *application dispositions*: we cannot be said to have a full grasp of a name unless we have a definite disposition to apply it or to withhold it under whatever conceivable changes the bearer of the name might come to undergo.[13] The ultimate test of whether we understand a name is whether we know, in principle, when and when not to apply it to an object. This should be a point on which all theories of names agree. Of course we can easily be in epistemic circumstances that prevent us from accurately exercising our mastery of the name, but that is beside the point. Someone who truly has a full grasp of the name and is asked to consider a possibility

---

[12] Thus Venus would no longer exist. But it might be appropriate, at some future time, to think intuitively that Venus had come back into being, say if the cloud resulting from the explosion coalesced into a planet and regained something like the original orbit.

[13] People who do not fully grasp a name may nevertheless use it successfully, as when they ask questions like 'What is Barolo?'.

in which its bearer undergoes a certain conceivable change will know whether that object continues to merit the name.

Suppose this much is accepted. And suppose further that the preponderance of speakers who use a given name and are capable of regular, successful use of it in a variety of circumstances, do fully grasp the name. Let's call them the *stewards* of the name. Then we may say, roughly, that the *category* of a name is the narrowest and 'most natural' property, among those its bearer actually instantiates, that the object would also instantiate in every counterfactual case in which the stewards of the name are disposed to continue to apply it.

To illustrate, consider Daffy. In every situation in which the stewards would continue to apply 'Daffy', the object is a *statue*. But it is also true that in every such situation it would be a *physical object* and (let us assume) a *twenty-first century American statue*, a *statue sculpted by so and so*, and so forth. But the first category is broader than *statue* and the latter are 'less natural'. They are less natural because none of them is the property we would be intuitively inclined to choose to categorize the object if asked, using the name, *what sort of thing* the object is. (The property one would be disposed to choose is of course *statue*.) So the category of a name is, in effect, the property we would choose to categorize the bearer, for an uninformed inquirer, from among those in the intersection of the classes of properties the object would instantiate in those counterfactual cases in which we would be disposed to continue to apply the name.[14]

What, then, are the categories of the names in our examples? The first three seem easy. The category of 'Daffy' is *statue*; the category of 'Château Margaux' is *château*; and the category of 'Donald Trump' is *human being* (or *person*). The case of

---

[14] Obviously names differ greatly in how widely they are used, with names of the famous having far greater circulation than those of the obscure. The stewards of a given name may thus be a tiny minority of the speakers of the language, and no doubt there are not many names whose stewards comprise a majority of speakers of the name's language of origin.

'Venus' is less straightforward. I believe case (1) shows that the category is not *physical object* (or *mereological sum*). It has to be narrower. And case (2) shows, perhaps surprisingly, that it is not *planet*. Venus might cease to be a planet and still merit the name 'Venus'. The category of 'Venus' is thus something like *good-sized celestial body* or perhaps merely *well integrated, good-sized physical object*. It is very important to see that this would hold even if Venus had been named in an official ceremony in which the name-giver had said something like, 'Let "Venus" be a name of yonder *planet*'.

These reflections strongly suggest that the category of an ordinary name is not determined by the name-giver. Instead, and roughly, it is determined by the application dispositions of the community of speakers. These dispositions dictate how the name is actually applied or withheld, including counterfactually, but they also govern the full range of unconsidered counterfactual possibilities. Now I'll offer a few more examples to help reinforce this claim.

(1) Suppose the name-giver had instead said 'Let "Venus" be a name of yonder *star*', intending 'star' in the astronomical sense and not as a synonym for 'celestial body'. If it were up to the name-giver to determine the category of a name, then this would not have been a successful naming at all since Venus isn't a star. But this flies in the face of the fact that 'Venus' would have been applied to the object with seeming success by millions of subsequent speakers (both before and after the discovery that Venus isn't a star). A theory that holds the seeming success of these millions of (imagined) uses to have been illusory is not credible.

(2) Another sort of case that favors the present view is this. We may introduce the name of a dog (or person, etc.) while invoking the category *puppy* (or *baby*). But we don't think a *new* naming is in order when the puppy matures beyond puppyhood. Nor is it credible to hold that there has been a tacit renaming.

(3) Also compelling, I believe, is the fact that a name-giver need not invoke any category at all in giving a name. With a doomed bottle of Champagne in hand, Donald Trump may simply say, 'I hereby christen thee "The Trumpanic"'. He may be *thinking* of the object in a certain way, perhaps as a *trophy*, but it is hard to believe that an unexpressed thought could take precedence over subsequent social use in determining the category. That use, of course, would seem to dictate that the category of the unfortunate name was *ship*.

(4) Further, I believe names can enter the language without benefit of any explicit naming. Suppose you bring home a puppy and start agonizing about names. You entertain many possibilities, look at books of popular dog names, discuss it with family and friends, but never settle on a name. In the meantime, while tossing potential names around, and without any explicit introduction, you call the puppy 'Rex' (or even 'Puppy'). When people ask what the puppy's name is, you respond by saying, 'Well, he doesn't really have a name yet, but I've been calling him "Rex"'. Surely this is wrong. The puppy's name is 'Rex' even if a new name will soon replace it. It is arguable, against this view, that the first episode of your calling him 'Rex' counts as an explicit naming. But either way we still have a name entering the language without appeal to any category.

(5) Certain names of geological formations and astronomical bodies may have their roots in prehistoric times. Such names began as sequences of sounds and their current manifestations may or may not resemble the originals very closely. It is difficult to believe that such names were introduced in explicit naming events. Much more likely is that what were initially merely *in*definite descriptions ('Cloudy Mountain') 'hardened' into names as a result of being applied exclusively to a single entity. The categories of such names would include *mountain*, *lake*, *celestial body*, and so forth. So here we again seem to have names without name-givers, and hence without appeal to any category.

Case (1)—the 'star' case—evidently shows that we may have a successful naming even if an incorrect category is invoked. Case (2)—the puppy case—shows that the explicitly invoked category need not be the real category. Case (3)—the 'Trumpanic' case—shows that there need be no category explicitly invoked in a naming, and case (4)—the 'Rex' case—(on one interpretation) shows that there needn't even be a naming in the first place. (On the variant interpretation it's simply another case of a naming with no category invoked.) Case (5)—the 'Cloudy Mountain' case—reinforces the speculation in case (4).

Collectively, I believe these cases strongly support the view advanced above: the category of an ordinary name is determined by the application dispositions of speakers in the linguistic community as a whole. I call this the *social determination* view. It is a very 'naturalistic' view—one that meshes well with the idea that the meanings of our words are determined by how we use them. According to this view, *naming is a shared activity in which the name-giver (or initial name-user), if there is one, does part of the work and society at large does the rest: the name-giver picks the name and the bearer, and the community as a whole determines the category.*

A natural question to ask about this view is whether it is really correct that typical names have stewards. What if seemingly competent and regular users of a name differ in their application dispositions (or have no such dispositions) in some counterfactual (or even actual) cases? We have, in effect, projected our conclusions about categories from a scant handful of cases. Further, it may not be entirely clear that the categories we have attached to names even in the seemingly straightforward examples above are beyond dispute. Perhaps there are cases that favor a reconsideration of those initially thought to be clear. We will take up these matters in the next section.

In adopting the social determination view I don't mean to claim that a name-giver never has the power to determine the category. I only insist that this doesn't happen in the case of *ordinary* names. When it does happen, the resulting name is a *technical* term, not an ordinary name. Thus, for a rather artificial example, there might be reasons for astronomers to name planets in the category *planet*. When such a name creeps into common use, as many technical terms do, there are two possibilities. First, it could be that ordinary use is sensitive to the unusual category. Then we would have ordinary speakers using technical terms more or less correctly. Second, it could be that the name is used as if its category were the one we would expect of a similar ordinary name. It is natural to think that initial such uses would simply be incorrect. But if the usage gained a foothold it would probably be best to say that a new ordinary name, lexically indistinguishable from the technical one, had seeped into general use. It would be yet another case of a name entering the language with no name-giver and so with no category explicitly invoked.

A special case of technical names is important in philosophy. We are able to introduce names that 'designate rigidly' in the (weak) sense that they are incapable of having distinct bearers between different contexts of use. For example, I might introduce the name 'O' in the presence of Daffy by pointing and saying, 'Let "O" be a (technical) name of that *physical object*'. The category of 'O' is then *physical object*.[15] With 'O' thus in place, I could make the earlier points against DR theories of *ordinary* names by noting that although *Daffy* could have been made of different matter, *O* could not, and that although Daffy is essentially a statue, O is not, etc.

We are also able to introduce names that *refer directly* to their bearers, but of course I deny that this is what we do with ordinary names. But I do think this is the best way to understand names of abstract entities like numbers and properties, and I

---

[15] Note that *physical object* is a very unlikely category for an *ordinary* name because it is so broad.

already exploited this above in capturing the great divide in a semi-formal way. It will emerge that whether we view such names as having categories is insignificant since they do not *express* them even if they have them. Moreover, their bearers are incapable of ceasing to be numbers, properties, etc. Directly referential technical names will play an important role in what follows.

Another case in which a name-giver *seems* to have categorial power is when someone names a thing of a category for which there is no antecedent practice of giving names. For example we might name attached parts of familiar objects such as rungs of ladders and handles of cheese graters. If your family members misread you and start calling the cheese grater by the name of its handle, this doesn't override your intentions because, after all, you do have the power to determine the *bearer*, and the bearer *isn't* a cheese grater. You are right to correct them, and their subsequent use might contribute to future category determination if similar names were to become common in the future.

The mere fact that typical ordinary names have categories provides an apparent challenge to the DR account, one that SD accounts needn't face because they give *meanings* to names, and the meanings may incorporate the categories. But how do we reconcile the DR theory with the fact that a named object may (intuitively) cease to belong to the category of its name? It might be thought that when Daffy is reshaped into a cube it is still the bearer of 'Daffy' on the DR account since it's intuitively the same object.[16]

---

[16] Of course this is one of the main sources of trouble for the DR view. As suggested earlier, a DR theorist might reject the intuition, putting a different conception in its place. But such a conception would not be so much an intuition as a metaphysical theory about 'physical objects'. Although such theories are surely possible, DR theorists have typically not offered them, and I remain very inclined to think that the intuition that the cube is 'the same physical object' would remain untouched. Such a theory would to this extent be counterintuitive, and thus would require further support in order to seem credible.

A DR theorist might respond as follows: 'We need to stop thinking intuitively and take seriously our commitment to perdurantism. We also need to recall Kripke's distinction between using a description to fix the referent (or bearer) of a name and using a description to give the meaning of a name. When we do these two things we get the following picture. The name-giver invokes the category *statue* in determining the bearer of "Daffy". As a result the name picks out a four-dimensional worm that is in fact a statue. The temporal extent of this worm is of course unknown at the time of the naming. But it is nevertheless *this* object that is loaded into propositions expressed with the help of "Daffy". There is a *longer* spacetime worm that contains this worm as a proper part and whose later slices have a cubical shape. That longer worm is *not* a statue, and so it isn't the worm that is loaded into these propositions. Because categories are used to help affix names to their bearers, the possibility of a named object ceasing to belong to the right category is thus eliminated.'

The problem with this picture is that it puts the determination of the category back into the hands of the name-giver and hence departs from the way names are actually used. We would have the potential consequence that, say, 'Venus' is not really a name (because the 'naming' invoked *star*). Or the potential consequence that, officially, 'Venus' doesn't apply after it is dragged out of orbit (because the naming invoked *planet*, and hence only applied to the part of the actual Venus-worm that was in orbit). It is also clear that this remedy doesn't help with the original composition-based objections to DR that were given in Section I.

4. Categories Redux

Simple generalizations about natural language have a good chance of being incorrect, and that is why I hedged the central claim of the previous section. While the vast majority of ordinary names seem to have straightforward, socially determined categories, there are cases that may seem less clear in one way or another, and may even prompt us to revise our thinking about the other cases. In this section we will look at a few less straightforward cases.

One is a case of radical error. Suppose an elaborate plot results in the surreptitious replacement of a cloned human by a superficially indistinguishable android. The cloning scientists give the name 'Susie' to the android thinking it is the human triumph of their expertise. The name spreads into the community in the usual way. Eventually a large number of people are using the name, successfully applying it to the android, and thinking Susie is a human being. Does this universal but mistaken conviction conflict with the doctrine of socially determined categories?

I don't believe so. The scientists have exercised their linguistic prerogative by affixing the name to the android despite the fact that they believe it is a human being. And community use determines that the category of 'Susie' is not *human being* because speakers are disposed to apply the name to what is *in fact* not a human being.

All speakers have a general disposition *not* to apply a name that was originally applied to an android, to a human (and vice versa, etc.). That the users believe Susie is a human being is a misleading but irrelevant fact. If the subterfuge is later exposed, people will react by concluding *that Susie isn't human after all*, not by concluding that Susie doesn't exist. So the intuitive conclusion is that the category of 'Susie' is *android*. This case is actually rather similar to the 'Venus'/'star' case considered above. Both suggest that community determination is not a matter of community *belief*, but rather a matter strictly of application dispositions. Given that Susie, an android, is the bearer of the name, the stewards of the name are disposed to apply it to what is in fact an android, and to continue to do so if and when the alarming discovery is made.

Another potentially touchy case is one in which categories may appear to drift.[17] Suppose there is a popular restaurant named 'The Palm'. The owners decide to put a slot machine in the waiting area. The machine gets lots of play and the restaurant continues to prosper. But the machine is making so much easy money that the owners decide to increase the size of the 'waiting area' at the expense of restaurant seating, adding more gambling opportunities. Many people are now frequenting The Palm without dining, and the owners are making ever more money. They decide to cut back to a very minimal food operation and let gambling dominate the business. We may imagine that ultimately The Palm no longer offers food and the entire space is given over to gambling. What was once a restaurant is now a casino, but everyone has been calling the establishment *The Palm* all along and with no sense of oddity.

This example is hardly far-fetched because just this sort of *functional* transformation—in this case a transformation in how something is *used*—actually does occur from time to time. (Many elaborate *residences*, for example including some famous châteaux of the Loire, have become what are now basically *museums*, and some changes of this sort can be gradual.) Does this call for a liberalization of the category doctrine so that categories of names may change over time? Or should we reconsider the notion of tacit renamings?

People who use 'The Palm' now include some who know the history and some who do not. The former will sometimes inform the latter by saying, for example, 'The Palm has been here for many years; in the old days it was a restaurant'. Intuitively, this is correct. But if 'The Palm' has undergone

---

[17] I thank Steve Reber for this example and for helpful comments on other topics treated in this book.

a category shift from *restaurant* to *casino*, then it cannot be correct, for the current bearer of the name will be a spacetime worm that does not include a segment that was a restaurant. Similarly, people who long ago said, 'As long as these owners don't sell, you can count on getting a good meal at The Palm', said something that is intuitively false. But if, at the time, the category had been *restaurant*, it need not have been false. We simply cannot retain the idea that 'The Palm' is *the same name* while letting its category drift. Under perdurantism, the different categories would force different bearers, so there would really be two or more names in play. So the notion of drifting categories is not defensible.

The natural conclusion to draw here, perhaps initially surprising, is that the category of the name 'The Palm' is something like *establishment* (or *institution*).[18] This is similar to the earlier conclusion that the category of 'Venus' isn't *planet*. But, of course, if the category of 'The Palm' was *establishment* all along, then it would not have been *restaurant* even if the owners had never changed a thing. We must conclude that, like *planet*, *restaurant* is not a potential category for an ordinary name, and we need to consider the possibility that no property that involves a significant *functional* component—whether involving use or other types of contingent extrinsic relations to other things—can be the category of a name. This suspicion will be reinforced below. The fact is that in cases like these we are disposed to continue applying names to things that undergo dramatic changes in function, and there are compelling reasons in such cases to think we are applying the same names, not new, lexically indistinguishable ones. (It is really true that *The Palm* was once a restaurant.)

But if *restaurant* and *planet* are not potential categories for names, can we be confident that, for example, *ship*, *statue*, and

---

[18] Notice that it isn't *building* (or *suite of rooms*, etc.) since The Palm could move to entirely different premises.

person really are potential categories for names? They can be categories only if the associated names would no longer apply to the bearers if they ceased to have these properties. So let's explore the matter a bit further.

The *Queen Mary* is a ship that has been permanently docked in Long Beach for about forty years. It hasn't sailed at all during this period and there is little chance that it will sail in the future. But it unquestionably remains a ship. On board there are restaurants, a hotel, and other attractions for tourists and the merely hungry, tired, or curious. The *Queen Mary* would still be a ship even if it had been permanently installed on dry land in Las Vegas and a casino had been added to the other on-board facilities. As long as the physical object itself remains unmodified in certain crucial respects, it remains a ship. It would take significant structural change to make that object cease to be a *ship*. It seems that no amount of change in everyday *function* could do it. (Thus part of being a ship may be having the capacity of sailing, but actually sailing is not part of this concept. Surely there have been ships that never sailed.) In the Château Margaux case we concluded that a certain bizarre reassembly of the parts of the château would render the (existing) name 'Château Margaux' inapplicable. The same conclusion seems to hold here, with the apparent consequence that the category of '*Queen Mary*' is *ship*. (Likewise, the category of the names of the Loire châteaux is *château* (or *castle*), not *residence*.)

It is not easy to see how Daffy could cease to be a statue without undergoing a significant rearrangement of its parts. But what if it acquired a significantly different physical relation to other objects? If Daffy were suspended by wire in the middle of a large plywood box and concrete were poured into the box and allowed to set, it seems to me that Daffy would still exist but would not be easily recovered for viewing. (People would say, 'We need to figure out the best way to recover Daffy without damaging it', etc.) I believe this would be true even if the surrounding medium were clay of the same sort, so that intact recovery would be much more difficult. The statue would, at least in principle, be recoverable. It would still be 'in there'. Thus it seems to me that *being a statue* is not a functional property in the present (admittedly somewhat vague) sense. It is rather a partly structural, partly intentional property.

I also think it's possible for Daffy to survive a decline of civilization in which no tradition of statuary survived but English was still spoken. Benighted archaeologists of the era might discover (say from its nameplate) that the item bore the name 'Daffy' while having no idea what its purpose had been. What then should we say if they proceeded to call the object 'Daffy'? I believe that at first they would be using the original name and applying it successfully to the object, but without fully grasping the name because they would lack the application dispositions of the long gone stewards of the name. But unfortunately these name users would not be in a position to ascend to stewardship. Instead, new application dispositions would begin to solidify as a result of ongoing counterfactual reflection (or reflection on actual changes the object might undergo), so that a new name with a new category would emerge. At the same time the original name, with its original category, would still correctly apply to Daffy, though lamentably there would be no one there who might apply it.

Let's take another look at the Trump/zombie case. I claimed that the category of the name was *person* (or *human being*). But we understood the case as one in which Trump had become a 'philosophical' zombie, and there is no way for anyone to tell that such a change has taken place. Then people will call the zombie 'Donald Trump', so shouldn't the social determination view yield a conclusion like the one we reached in the case of The Palm? The transformation would not be gradual, but that shouldn't really matter. (The owners of The Palm could have made it a casino overnight with the result still The Palm.)

Shouldn't we then conclude that the category of 'Donald Trump' was never *person*, but rather one that encompasses both human and zombie (etc.), and hence that none of our *own* names has that category?

I believe the answer is no. The reason was present in the Susie case. Speakers have a general disposition *not* to apply a name that was originally applied to a person, to a zombie. The current users, if somehow apprised of the undiscoverable fact, or in considering such a circumstance counterfactually, would concede that the ultimate entity is not Trump. In the situation as it stands, however, they *are* applying 'Trump' to a zombie, and with apparent success. The intuitive conclusion should be that in this bizarre case there has been an unwitting but genuine introduction of a new, lexically indistinguishable name. The category of this name is of course *zombie* (and the name has a different bearer). Properties like *person*, *zombie*, and *android* are at bottom structural in nature, and have no crucial functional component. I believe this is the key difference between the Trump, Susie, and also the Daffy and *Queen Mary* cases, on the one hand, and the cases of The Palm and Venus, on the other.[19]

Thus I think our original intuitions about the categories of names like 'Venus', 'Daffy', and 'Donald Trump' are compatible with the doctrine of categories and social determination. A nagging question, mentioned above, is whether there really are stewards. Is it true that speakers who unquestionably have a genuine command of a name in actual practice also have the very same application dispositions?

Let's return for a final time to the original two-pronged Venus case. I claimed that the category had to be something

---

[19] In the cases of Daffy and the *Queen Mary*, where the categories of the names are *statue* and *ship*, there is an extra wrinkle, which is that they are artifacts and hence that their categories have an undeniably intentional component. But the relevant intentions explicitly involve the structures of the objects that ultimately come to belong to these categories.

narrower than *physical object* but wider than *planet*, and suggested either *good-sized celestial body* or *well-integrated, good-sized physical object*. Why the difference? The reason, unstated at the time, was this. A large spherical boulder on the surface of the earth does not count as a celestial body. Venus, having abandoned its orbit, might gently come to rest on the surface of an astonishingly large planet in some other solar system. In that environment it would merely be a large spherical boulder. In fact I believe that savvy users of 'Venus' would continue to call this object 'Venus' and that there would be no good reason to think they were using a new, lexically indistinguishable name with a new category (and bearer). The ultimate natural history of Venus would include the stretch of time when it was just a huge boulder. If this is right, then the appropriate category for 'Venus' really is *well integrated, good-sized physical object* (or something very close to that). Although it may not be obvious at first, *celestial body* is like *planet* in having a definite functional component. A celestial body must be more or less surrounded by space. Consider the object that is all of Venus except for its outermost, meter-thick 'shell'. Intuitively, it is neither a planet nor a celestial body. The reason has to do with its relations to other objects. It isn't functioning either as a planet or as a celestial body. It is merely a large part of something that is functioning in both ways.

It would be rather surprising if the application dispositions of experienced users of typical names diverge in unconsidered counterfactual cases, but without our having noticed divergences either in actual application or in explicit counterfactual consideration. If there are no cases of actual or explicit counterfactual divergence, then that is considerable evidence that there are no hidden divergences. But in actual and explicit counterfactual cases, I think a little reflective discussion always tends to align what might first have seemed to be divergences.

But suppose this sunny view is wrong and there really are irreconcilable divergences in some cases. One case might be just like the Venus/boulder case, but with one camp insisting that Venus ceased to exist when it became a big boulder, the other taking the view I actually think experienced speakers would take. Then I believe the natural conclusion would be that in this case the two camps really are using different names, of course with different categories, and that the members of each camp are stewards of their own name 'Venus'. An inelegant consequence would be that what seem to be everyday uses of a single name actually are not. But in practice this would not be that bad because the two names would have the same bearer and there would be no disagreement about the bearer's actual properties or about the preponderance of its intuitive modal properties. This is a consequence we can live with if there really are such differences.

5. A Theory of Names with Bearers

On the present theory, the category of a name plays a central role in the semantic contribution it makes in sentences in which it occurs. Since the direct reference account has been rejected, the new proposal will give names *meanings* but, since definite-description accounts have also been rejected, these will not be meanings that are expressed by definite descriptions (whether 'rigidified' or not).

On the present proposal, a name *expresses* a property involving its category, and we will think of this property as the *meaning* of the name. A given *use* of a name of course occurs in a specific context, and the occurrence of the name in that context also contributes a *quantifier* (along with the expressed property) to the intuitive proposition expressed by the sentence token. I'll now attempt to illustrate how this works in a straightforward case. But doing so requires a little preliminary groundwork of a slightly reformatory nature. We will work with the sentence 'George W. Bush is a Republican'.

As we discussed earlier, in our early undergraduate days in first-order logic classes we were taught to translate this sentence into the language of logic by a formula like 'Rb', where the predicate letter 'R' formally represents the predicate 'is a Republican' and the individual constant 'b' formally represents the name 'George W. Bush'. Then, a little later, we were trained to *interpret* 'R' and 'b' by assigning a set of individuals to 'R' and an individual to 'b'. After that we learned a general definition a consequence of which is that the present formula is *true with respect to the interpretation* iff the individual assigned to 'b' is a member of the set assigned to 'R'. Soon we were also encouraged to *think* of the set assigned to 'R' as representing the *property* of being a Republican. This last, extra-semantical advice was designed to relieve anxiety in students who realized there is nothing in the official semantics to prevent the simultaneous assignment of the same set of individuals to *different* predicate letters. It was aimed at helping them *pretend* that 'Rb' and (say) 'Ab' have different 'meanings' in the semantics, when of course they do not. Savvy students' anxieties on this point went unrelieved.

There are several serious problems with this early training. One is of course its extensionality, as just suggested. It would have been philosophically better, though at the price of an extra layer of complexity, to have assigned *properties* to interpret predicate letters, and then to have assigned *extensions* to properties.[20] Truth conditions might continue to be given *via* extensions, but we would no longer have to pretend that 'Rb' and 'Ab' had different meanings in the semantics since they truly would. A second problem with the extensional semantics (not relieved by the reform just mentioned) is that the truth-conditions, when true, are *necessarily* true whereas the translated English sentences generally are not. George W. Bush is not

---

[20] Or we could assign ordered pairs of properties and extensions to predicates, etc.

necessarily a Republican, but if he's a member of a certain specific set, then this circumstance is of course necessary.[21]

A yet more important problem for present purposes is that the extensional semantics carries a heavy bias toward a DR philosophy of *ordinary* names. After all, an individual constant like 'b' is supposed to play the role of a *name* like 'George W. Bush'. If, in first-order logic, we *interpret* 'b' merely by assigning an individual to it, this encourages us to think that perhaps the 'meaning' of an ordinary name like 'George W. Bush' is in turn just an individual or, perhaps, that it has no meaning, only reference.

Ironically, the very apparatus of first-order logic was initially developed in order to serve as a precise language for formalizing *mathematics*, where a DR understanding of names is perfectly defensible.[22] But George W. Bush is not an abstract object and it is metaphysically jarring to be told that he or any other concrete entity is a constituent of any genuine *propositions* at all since they are supposed to be abstract entities.[23] Surely any theory of

---

[21] This criticism might seem a bit picky and unfair because matters are remedied when the extensional semantics is generalized into the possible-worlds framework. But this impression wouldn't really be right because even in that framework the truth-condition for what is a contingent fact in a given 'world' is a necessary fact—the fact that a certain entity belongs to a certain set. The truth-condition is *not* that a certain entity belongs to a certain set *and* there are other sets assigned to the predicate letter with respect to different 'worlds' to which the entity does not belong. The entity's non-membership in those sets is of course just as necessary as its membership in the relevant world's truth-condition-giving set. Here we have the other side of the coin of what I called (in Chapter 3) the fundamental weirdness of possible-worlds accounts of modality. There the weirdness was that what is necessary in a world depends on what goes on in other worlds. Here it is that what is contingent in a world likewise depends on what goes on in other worlds. There is a rock-bottom mismatch between the intuitive conception of possibility and necessity and the mathematical device of world theory.

[22] As suggested earlier, although I don't find it mandatory, I do think it's quite reasonable to think of a sentence like 'Five is prime' as expressing an (intuitive) proposition that contains the abstract mathematical object *five* as a constituent. Similarly for names of other sorts of *abstracta*.

[23] Of course we already saw that direct-reference theories automatically include concrete entities among the constituents of propositions. Perhaps the most

propositions that builds them entirely of abstract ingredients has a heavy initial advantage over one that allows concrete constituents.[24] But even without propositions, it would be perfectly reasonable to think that the 'meaning' of 'five' is simply its abstract bearer, or that it had a *referent* but no 'meaning'. But I believe it's unreasonable to think that the meaning of 'George W. Bush' is a concrete object (or that it merely refers to that object and has no meaning). This point was already made elaborately in Section 1, with the examples of 'Daffy' and 'Venus'.

Here I am not objecting to first-order syntax itself, only to its typical deployment in representing ordinary language. I am, of course, objecting to extensional semantics. As an historical complaint, I think the application to ordinary English of a formal semantical framework initially designed for mathematics took place without adequate attention to its philosophical appropriateness, and all too soon became deeply entrenched. It has been misleading us ever since. At the same time, I believe it is now very common for philosophers to recognize the inadequacy of extensional semantics for interpreting ordinary language, and hence that the present objection to the extensionality is neither original nor surprising. But I now want to offer a new way of bringing our logic to bear on language involving ordinary proper names.

---

sophisticated recent theory in which propositions have concrete constituents is that of King (2007), and here the concrete constituents appear as a consequence of an explicit assumption of direct reference. But King's project is best seen as an account of how propositional constituents are tied together into unitary entities *whatever* those constituents might be like ontologically, so I believe he really has no ultimate commitment to concrete constituency. As I understand him, the direct reference is serving as a convenient simplifying assumption for the purpose of pursuing the overall structural project. He expresses sympathy for the assumption but does not try to defend it. See King (2007: 6–7).

[24] I don't mean to be committing myself to any theory of propositions here since I actually reject them. (See Jubien (2001b).) This point is for those who do see propositions as the meanings of certain sentences or sentence-tokens.

A Theory of Names with Bearers

A typical sincere utterance of 'George W. Bush is a Republican' would carry with it 'existential presuppositions' (or 'existential import') and the speaker would accordingly be 'ontologically committed' to Bush. But not every sincere utterance of this sentence need automatically have existential import. A shipwrecked person might read an account of Bush's presidency, dropped from a passing airplane, and take it to be a work of *fiction*. But then if he later utters the sentence to a fellow castaway in an effort to inform her about (what he takes to be) the central character of the work, he does so without existential import. He doesn't believe there really is such a person as George W. Bush, but his utterance is nevertheless *true*—neither he nor it is 'committed' to the existence of Bush.[25] Thus, and without further motivation, I will assume that whether or not existential presuppositions are present is strictly a function of *context*—it isn't determined by the semantics of the proper names themselves.

So different utterances of our sample sentence may express different (intuitive) propositions in different contexts, so that there is no single canonical way to translate the sentence into the language of logic—notably not 'Rb'!—so as to capture a mythical *unique* proposition that would be expressed by an arbitrary utterance. But now let's consider a sincere utterance of the sentence by someone who knows that George W. Bush really does exist, in a context with nothing fancy to defeat the existential presupposition. On the present view, such an utterance expresses the (intuitive) proposition *that something instantiates both (the property of) being George W. Bush and (the property of) being a Republican*.[26] Thus, when it is useful to do

---

[25] Think also of conversations between parents and children 'about Santa Claus'. The children's utterances have existential presuppositions; the parents' do not. The topics of existential presuppositions and ontological commitment are subtle and will not be treated in detail here.

[26] It is important to notice that in this treatment the 'semantics' does not reflect the intuitive grammatical distinction between subject and predicate. When

so, I will translate the original English into the language of first-order logic by the formula

$$\exists x(Ixb \ \& \ Ixr),$$

where 'I' represents and is interpreted by the instantiation relation, and 'b' and 'r' are individual constants interpreted as referring directly to the *properties* of *being George W. Bush* and *being a Republican*.[27] Further, I will take the quantifier as ranging over *arbitrary physical objects* (setting aside worries about dualism in the interest of simplicity) *and abstract entities* (or perhaps over a restricted range of such entities). Although the individual constants for properties have been interpreted extensionally, the overall semantical treatment is not extensional because 'I' is interpreted by a genuine *relation*, not (e.g.) by a set of ordered pairs, and because 'Ixp' is defined to be true (for an assignment) under the interpretation iff the individual assigned to 'x' instantiates the *property* denoted by 'p' (and also because *sets* play no role in the semantics).

The first thing to notice about the (intuitive) proposition captured by the interpreted formula is that it has no specific physical object as an (intuitive) constituent. Instead it has two

---

subjects are ordinary proper names I believe this is the inevitable result of the rejection of direct reference.

[27] Notice also that this departure from classroom logic has a very important consequence for our understanding of so-called *identity sentences*, for a sentence like 'Mark Twain is Samuel Clemens' will not be translated to a formula like 't = c'. It will go, first, into '$\exists x \exists y(Ixt \ \& \ Iyc \ \& \ x = y)$'. But this is equivalent to '$\exists x(Ixt \ \& \ Ixc)$', raising the suspicion that in no reasonable sense is the original English an 'identity sentence', as they have typically been conceived. The discussion of various 'problems of identity' has unfortunately been dominated by the presupposition that it is legitimate to translate ordinary proper names by individual constants of first-order logic. I believe the result has more often been confusion than illumination. Some have suggested that in such sentences the 'is' is not the 'is' of identity, but rather the 'is' of predication. See, e.g., Fred Sommers (1969), and also Michael Lockwood (1975) who traces the idea to Mill. Tyler Burge (1973) has argued that proper names function semantically as predicates, which is an available way of construing the idea that they express properties in the way I am suggesting here.

properties, one rather special, the other rather ordinary. So the proposition is not *singular* with respect to the bearer of the name 'George W. Bush'. The special property is of course the property of *being George W. Bush*, which is none other than Bush's person-essence, given that the category of the name is *person* (or *human being*). The considerations of Sections 3 and 4 point directly to this conclusion and I will assume it is correct from now on.

Let's consider this in a little more detail. Even independently of the apparatus of k-essences, I believe it is just an empirical fact that we speak and behave as if there were such properties as *being Bush*, so I find appealing to such a property no more alarming than appealing to *being human*. It is equally clear, I believe, that we speak and behave as if such properties as *being Bush* are *singulary*, because we simply do not allow that there could be more than one George W. Bush (etc.).

I also think it's just a fact that we speak and act as if nothing could be Bush—could be that very human being—without having certain properties. To put it intuitively, we think that certain properties are *essential to Bush*. When asked whether Bush might have had such and such property we are generally prepared to offer an opinion or at least to think the question makes sense and merits an answer. First and foremost, I assume that we think nothing could be Bush without being human. This is one of the legitimate lessons of Kripkean thought experiments and it is built into the present analysis of modal notions. We may be expected to disagree as to exactly which properties are essential to him. But this should initially come as no surprise since we routinely disagree about exactly what it takes even to be *human* or to be a *ship*, etc. Just as terms like 'human' (and 'ship', etc.) are vague, so is 'George W. Bush'—at the very least it inherits the vagueness of 'human'. It is easier to get a grip on *being Bush* if we idealize and pretend ordinary words and phrases aren't vague. We do this by pretending that ordinary, seemingly property-denoting and property-expressing phrases really do denote and express *specific* and precise properties (and not clusters or families of properties, not mysterious 'vague' or 'fuzzy' properties, etc.). While no ultimate account of natural language can avoid coming to grips with the problem of vagueness, it would be a major distraction to try to deal with it here, and I think it will be clear in the end that nothing important is prejudiced by the idealization.

But even idealizing to this extent, there remains room for philosophical disagreement about what's essential to Bush — that is, about exactly which precise property 'George W. Bush' expresses. Some people (I believe including Bush) will hold that this property entails *having an immortal and immaterial soul* while others will deny it. Yet others will claim it entails *having such and such DNA sequence* while others deny it. Some will say it entails *being male* or at least *originally being male*. Some may say it is simply the property of *being such and such specific physical object* while others (including myself) deny this. It is clearly true that the actual use (including counterfactual use) of proper names of people doesn't settle precisely what property is expressed by such a name because that use will actually be inconsistent across the field of use, as the present examples reveal. The fact remains that *we speak and act as if there were such a property even as we disagree about its exact nature, and the same is true of virtually any ordinary property we might happen to consider.*[28] Thus I suggest that we abstract away from such philosophical disagreements and ignore them just as we've agreed to ignore vagueness. Nothing that follows here will depend on claims about philosophically controversial entailments of properties like *being Bush*.

Under this double idealization, there is then a single property that 'George W. Bush' expresses.[29] Intuitively, to repeat,

---

[28] As just noticed, we disagree on whether *being human* entails *having a soul*.

[29] My own view, quite beside the present point, is that person-essences are heavily biological. They involve our originating zygotes. A consequence is that

A Theory of Names with Bearers

this property may be thought of as the conjunction of whatever properties an entity has to have in order to be George W. Bush.[30] It's the 'essence' of that *person*, the totality of what is entailed by *being that person*. We are now in a position to give a two-part, general statement of the view I've been describing so far:

> *1. For each ordinary proper name n, there is a unique kind k such that k is the category of n and n expresses a k-essence. 2. Let n be an (arbitrary) ordinary proper name. Then an occurrence of a subject-predicate sentence with subject term n, where the context requires existential presuppositions, expresses the (intuitive) proposition that something (or other) instantiates both of the properties N and P, where N is the k-essence expressed by n and P is the property expressed by the predicate.*

We have arrived at this view with the help of an example using a name that has a bearer, but I hope it will become clear that nothing really depends on this circumstance. I believe that typical 'empty' names are just as 'ordinary' as typical names that have bearers, and that they function in essentially the same way. I will try to motivate this in the next chapter.

---

typical speakers do not know exactly what property a name like 'Bush' expresses. But typical speakers don't know exactly what properties terms like 'dog' or 'ship' express either.

[30] As explained in Chapter 4, this makes the property of *being Bush* seem heavily 'modal', and indeed it is. But so is any other nontrivial property since all nontrivial properties have nontrivial entailments.

6

FICTIONAL NAMES

In this chapter I will sketch a view according to which empty names function essentially the way names with bearers have been claimed to function. But I won't offer a comprehensive theory because the topic is very complicated and it isn't obvious that the picture I have in mind would apply straightforwardly in every conceivable case. What are intuitively 'names of fictional characters' provide the most common examples of empty names, and I will work with them exclusively. Restricting attention to 'fictional names' is convenient because the conditions of their introduction are relatively uniform and clear by comparison with those of mythological and other empty names.

As I see it, there are two central facts about fictional names. First, they express k-essences, and second, the k-essences they express have a special feature that sets them apart from those expressed by names that have bearers. If a fictional name expresses a k-essence, then the special feature is that its k-essence entails *being fictional*, and hence also *not existing*. (Entailment, of course, is transitive.) More will be said about this soon, but we now turn to the first claim.

1. K-essences and the 'Background' of the Story

I think three considerations together favor the idea that fictional names express k-essences. First, as I've already insisted, ordinary *nonempty* names like 'George W. Bush' express k-essences. Second, and speaking very loosely and intuitively, typical fictional names (with notable exceptions) function like ordinary nonempty names 'within a work of fiction'. That is (in general) they function 'within the story' as if they had bearers and had been introduced in some appropriate way.[1] The third point merely reinforces the second. It is that writers of fiction almost never build into their stories principles about the functioning of names that might differ from those that actually prevail (whatever these may be). So if it's true that ordinary names express k-essences, then we should expect this of intuitive occurrences of fictional names 'within the story', unless it is explicit in the story that names function some other way. That uses of fictional names *outside* the story express k-essences will then follow from the fact that they are uses of the same names that, intuitively, occur 'within the story'.

The principle at work here is easier to illustrate than to state, but I think the driving intuition is very clear. Roughly, it is that every story has a nontrivial but inexplicit 'background'. Here is a simple illustration. Consider the nursery rhyme 'Jack and Jill'.[2] When we hear this rhyme it is legitimate for us to take certain things to be true that are not explicit. For example: that both characters are ambulatory, that Jack is a boy and Jill is a girl, that Jack sustains a head injury, and so on. But there is nothing in the letter of the verse that warrants *any* of this, notably the idea that Jack and Jill are young human beings. Yet they are. Somehow it is 'part of the story' that they are humans. But it isn't simply that the author intended them to be humans. In fact, I believe the author might have intended them to be aliens from outer space, and that this would not have

---

[1] Of course within a given story a fictional name from another story (even a fictional story) may be used as a *fictional* name, as when one character says of another, 'Inspector Floyd operates like Sherlock Holmes'.

[2] Here I will assume that the story was written by an earthbound human and intended for a human audience.

altered the fact that they are human beings. (We will return to this later.) That these characters are humans, I believe, is *socially determined* in much the same way that the category of a nonempty proper name like 'Venus' was held to be socially determined in Chapter 5. More will be said about this soon.

A story, if taken strictly at face value, generally does not tell us enough. It can only be a specific, coherent story if certain matters are taken for granted, in other words, if the story is assumed to be 'filled out' in certain ways. Certainly, when read or recited on Earth by humans, 'Jack and Jill' is going to be understood as a story 'about humans', and I believe this understanding is unquestionably correct, at least given that the author wrote it in English for earthly use.[3] This is akin to the fact that 'Venus' is going to be taken correctly to apply to a certain object even if it goes out of orbit.

Thus it is one of the definitive features of storytelling and story hearing that the hearer is entitled to assume 'normal' filling out unless the author explicitly builds something into the story that overrides it. The other side of this coin is that the storyteller cannot successfully depart from what would normally be assumed by the intended audience without making the departure explicit or, perhaps, tipping it off in some subtler way. So a story similar to 'Jack and Jill' but about space aliens could only be told (by one of *us*) if their alien nature were made explicit or at least hinted at in the story. Hence if the author of the actual 'Jack and Jill' conceived it all along as a story about space aliens, perhaps enjoying the conceit that the readers would get

---

[3] If the story was written by an alien on another planet and a copy somehow found its way to Earth, then it is not a story about humans, but one about aliens on another planet, written in a language relevantly indistinguishable from English. If the copy is found and initially assumed to have been written on Earth in English, it has been misconstrued. But if it subsequently seeps into our literature, then it has in effect been unwittingly translated into English and socially transformed into a story about humans. David Lewis develops two candidate analyses of what is 'true in a story' both of which accommodate truths that aren't explicit. One of them has a pronounced social component. See Lewis (1978).

it wrong, this is every bit as irrelevant as a name giver's invoking the category *planet* in naming Venus. In thinking it's a story about human children, the readers are getting it right because they are participating in a social institution that *makes* it right. That countless similar stories, not explicitly about humans, have been taken to be about humans, has established that the k-essences of the names of such characters entail *being human*.

Stories more complex than 'Jack and Jill' may require lots more filling out. For example, many stories contain explicit dialogue between characters. If the story is written in English and the dialogue on the page appears to be in English, we are entitled to assume it is English and to take it more or less at face value. We generally needn't entertain the possibility that the exchanges mean nothing like what they seem to mean—for example that they are coded messages (or that they are in alien-English, etc.)—unless there is something explicit in the story to provoke this suspicion.

Similarly, when what seem to be tokens of proper names appear in print on the page before us, we are entitled to assume that they *are* tokens of names, and that, 'within the story', the characters acquired these names in one or another of the normal ways of acquiring names, and moreover that these names function the way ordinary names do in actual life. If I am right that ordinary names in actual life express k-essences, then so do typical fictional names 'within' their respective stories. (If an author wants his fictional names to function in some alien way, for example as directly referential tags or as disguised rigidified definite descriptions, then it is up to him to build this into the story!)

Now, the only occasions on which fictional names are *actually* used are of course *not* 'within in the story'—they are used by actual people, notably by an author in writing the story and by readers in discussing it. But, intuitively, they are uses of the same names that the story establishes as *fictionally* used. Spread throughout the Sherlock Holmes stories, for example, there are many specific *fictional* uses of the name 'Holmes'. It is strictly *fictional* that any such uses took place. Since it is part of the filled-out fiction that these fictional uses express k-essences, and the extra-fictional uses are uses of the same names, it is difficult not to conclude that the extra-fictional uses—again, the only *actual* uses—express k-essences. But exactly what k-essences? We now begin to develop an answer to this question.

2. The Fictional Stance

I view fiction as a linguistic activity or institution whose hallmark is a pair of interlocking and cooperating *intentions* involving author (etc.) and reader (etc.). The first is the author's intention that the work *be* fiction. The second is the reader's intention to read it *as* fiction. On the present conception the author's intention is decisive: if a work is intended to be fiction, then it is fiction. But a part of the author's intention that it be fiction is that it be read as fiction, that is, the fiction is intended for readers who have the second of the cooperating intentions. The reader's intention involves a certain *attitude*, one that includes an effort to ignore, suspend, or otherwise 'screen off' the knowledge that what is being depicted is not factual. In a certain way the reader must *pretend* that what is depicted is factual despite knowing it isn't. I call this attitude of temporary benign self-deception the *fictional stance*. Thus fiction is seen as a kind of cooperative enterprise in which authors provide us with material for the imagination, and then we take this material and treat it in a certain special way by adopting the fictional stance. It is the fictional stance that makes our experience of fiction potentially so compelling. When we adopt it, we in effect insert ourselves into the story as unseen observers.[4]

---

[4] The present view of fiction is strongly influenced by Kendall Walton, who has elaborated and defended a similar conception in a number of places. For example see Walton (1978).

It is probably generally true that authors also adopt the fictional stance in writing their stories, but it doesn't seem necessary. An author might be acutely aware while writing that actual events are not being described and might even find it difficult to slip into the fictional stance. But there would still be the intention that the story be taken as fiction, that is, that readers adopt the fictional stance in reading it.

3. A Case Study

The last chapter of Raymond Chandler's *Farewell, My Lovely* begins with the sentence, 'It took over three months to find Velma'. This fictional observation clearly carries existential import. More precisely, it is fiction that such a remark was made (or thought) and also fiction that the occurrence of the name in that fictional remark bore existential import. But when we discuss the novel and say, for example, 'For a long time we don't even know whether Velma is still alive', there is no existential import since we know 'Velma' is an empty name. This is a remark we make from *outside* the fictional stance, but it is a remark *about* the flow of our thinking while reading the novel *in* the fictional stance.

I have emphasized that the only actual occurrences of 'Velma' are 'outside' the novel. These include the occurrences that appear on many pages of printed copies of the book, and they include the occurrences that appeared on sheets of paper that rolled out of Chandler's typewriter while he was writing the novel. Thus let's think for a moment about the token of 'It took over three months to find Velma' that in fact appears in ink on a brittle, yellowed page in my copy of the book. It is plainly *not* an occurrence of the sentence 'within the story'. It is rather an extra-fictional occurrence whose purpose is to convey a certain (intuitive) proposition to readers who have adopted the fictional stance. The proposition is *that there is someone who instantiates being Velma, and it took over three months to find that person.* The sentence-token on the page is intended to convey this proposition to readers so that they may pretend it is true. The token is not intended to *assert* the proposition, for the proposition makes a false existential claim. The intent is that the token merely *express* the proposition, so as to put it before the cooperative reader's imagination.

But we cannot get a good grip on this proposition without a better understanding of *being Velma*, which will take a little work to develop. I will begin by making several claims about this property. First, it is what I will call a *fictional-person*-essence, which I see *not* as a special case of a person-essence, but as a k-essence of its own special kind that will nevertheless be seen to function more or less like a typical person-essence. So the category of the name 'Velma' is *fictional person.* I believe that simply by intending his book to be fiction, and by introducing the name with the intention that it have no actual bearer, Chandler established (in a way that cannot be overridden by subsequent social use) that *being Velma* entails *being fictional*.[5] It is very likely that Chandler also intended Velma to be taken from within the fictional stance as a *person*. But I think this is irrelevant because it is socially determined that *being Velma* entails *being a person.* The determination takes place from within the fictional stance. Readers adopting the stance are going to take Velma to be a person just as we took Jack and Jill to be people, and this overrides any possible perverse authorial intentions. Whether explicit or not, it is part of the story that Velma is a person.

Being Velma is a perfectly genuine property, but it differs dramatically from real person-essences of actual people. Although it is part of the filled-out fiction that someone (likely

---

[5] Of course some of the entities that crop up in the novel are not fictional, for example Carole Lombard, Beverley Hills, Dartmouth College, and the Statue of Liberty.

unmentioned) introduced the name by attaching it to a bearer, in fact it was introduced by Chandler so as to have no bearer. As just emphasized, he *intended* 'Velma' to be the name of a *fictional* character. I attach great weight to this circumstance. I believe it has the consequence that *being Velma* not only isn't actually instantiated, it isn't even *possibly* instantiated.

Surely it was within Chandler's power to determine that Velma is fictional simply by intending it. And just as surely, no actual flesh-and-blood person is *fictional*, no matter what stories happen to have been written and no matter what things happen to exist. Hence a situation in which, say, *being Velma* was instantiated would be one in which a flesh-and-blood human being was *fictional*. But this is absurd. So there could be no situation in which *being Velma* was instantiated. In short, the property is necessarily uninstantiated.[6] A consequence is that works of fiction are not about specific metaphysically possible situations. A work of fiction isn't 'believable' or 'realistic' because *it* is possible, but rather because *something like it* is possible. The fiction itself is literally *impossible*.

From the present property-theoretic perspective on modality, the author's intention that Velma be fictional is reflected in the entailment of *being fictional* by the fictional-person-essence *being Velma*. We should of course also allow that *being Velma* entails *existing*, just as any property does, even those that could not be instantiated. (For example, *being round and square* entails *existing* because it entails *being round*, which of course entails *existing*.) Thus *being Velma* has contradictory entailments and as a result it is no surprise that it is necessarily uninstantiated.[7]

---

[6] This basic argument is given in greater detail in Jubien (1997: chapter 10). The position is similar to and perhaps even unconsciously inspired by Kripke's famous view about unicorns (Kripke, 1972, 1980: 23–4, 156–7). I don't accept his view about unicorns, but I remember being delighted when he mentioned it in the first *Naming and Necessity* lecture in 1970. The reason I reject the view will become clear in Chapter 7.

[7] We will return to the topic of necessary existence and necessary nonexistence in the next section.

Being Venus and *being Velma* differ not only because the latter entails *not existing* and the former does not. The former property is a k-essence whose relevant kind was socially determined once the bearer of the name was chosen by the name-giver. But in the latter case the author introduced the name and 'chose the bearer' by determining that there was none. Moreover, it is part of the filled-out fiction that someone other than the author introduced the name and did so with the aid of a bearer. Finally, it is part of the filled-out fiction that Velma isn't fictional, that she actually exists. So the name is actually introduced in a way that differs dramatically from how it is fictionally introduced. Is it really plausible, in the face of all these divergences, to hold that its occurrences express the same k-essence both 'within' and outside the story?

I believe the answer is yes. The basic reason is that there really are no occurrences of the name 'within the story'. What seem to be such occurrences are merely fictional. There was really only one introduction of the name, and Raymond Chandler was responsible for it. There are several legitimate ways for us to introduce names, and one of them is by writing works in which we intend it to be fiction that the name has a bearer. I claimed that when Chandler typed the sentence, 'It took over three months to find Velma', the token *expressed* a certain (intuitive) proposition. It was a proposition with clear existential import and hence false. But when we read the book, we are in the fictional stance and in our pretending or imagining we ignore this fact or otherwise screen it off. We do this in part by screening off the fact that *being Velma* entails *being fictional* (and hence *failing to exist*). We thus indulge in a fanciful *pretense* that 'Velma' expresses a real person-essence and has a bearer in the face of the fact that it does not and could not. The intuitive proposition that is actually expressed is of course necessarily false. On the other hand, in writing the sentence, Chandler surely doesn't *assert* this proposition.

Authors of fiction are not dealing out streams of *lies* or other *misrepresentations*, for there is no intent to deceive. They're engaging in a more complicated and subtle sort of linguistic activity, which we already commonly call *storytelling* (and less commonly *fictionalizing*). So *if* Chandler asserts anything at all in writing this sentence, it is the proposition *that it is part of his fiction that it took over three months to find Velma*. In this way he might be taken to be asserting something true. But such an assertion, since it is in part about Chandler, would not be an intuitive part of the fiction itself. Roughly speaking, on this account, every sentence of a novel is imbued with the fictive intentions of the novelist but without *thereby* expressing propositions that are partly about the novelist or about being fictional. Accordingly, to engage appropriately in the reading of fiction—to adopt the fictional stance—is to ignore what might be held to be *asserted* and to pretend that what is *expressed* is true even though generally it is not. What is expressed in this example is again merely the false proposition that something (or other) instantiates *being Velma* and that it took over three months to find that person. We adopt the fictional stance by pretending this expressed proposition is true and we do this by screening off our knowledge of its literal falsity, which partly requires pretending that *being Velma* lacks some of the entailments it actually has (notably *being fictional*). In effect we pretend the name expresses a person-essence rather than a fictional-person-essence. I believe this expression/assertion strategy also provides the key to understanding actual occurrences of 'Velma'—those outside the novel—so that we may see the name as functioning in a uniform way between its actual and merely fictional uses.[8]

We have not yet been entirely specific about the property of *being Velma*. Speaking intuitively, Velma's 'identity' is fixed by Chandler's descriptions of her features and role in the novel.

---

[8] There is more on the expression/assertion strategy in Jubien (1997: chapter 10).

These features and this role are what differentiate Velma from other characters in this and other works of fiction, and there is nothing else to go on. (Of course I am not suggesting that she cannot also appear in other works.) Let's assume that Chandler did not borrow Velma from some earlier work of his or someone else's. The property of *being Velma* is then one that is fixed forever by *Farewell, My Lovely* in accordance with Chandler's intentions and social determination from within the fictional stance. I suggest that it is the property of *being a fictional character that, from the fictional stance regarding Chandler's* Farewell, My Lovely, *instantiates a specific but unspecified person-essence and has such and such features and plays such and such role*. The relevant features and role are of course those that are intuitively 'attributed to Velma' in the (filled-out) novel. Should Velma make a subsequent appearance in another work, actual occurrences of 'Velma' in discussions of that work will still express this fictional-person-essence. In accordance with our earlier discussion it should be clear that it is impossible for this property to be instantiated.

There are at least four ways 'Velma' may occur outside the story. One arises when we correct someone's misapprehension by saying things like, 'Velma isn't real—she's a fictional character from a famous novel'. Another occurs when we talk about what is in the filled-out fiction but may be neither 'explicit' nor a logical consequence of what is 'explicit' ('Velma tried to escape her past'). A third sort of use happens when we go beyond the filled-out fiction and dabble in questions of literary interpretation ('Velma personifies fatalism'). The fourth, which we might call 'analogical', involves appealing to a character in discussing an actual situation. ('*Velma* would never have sung *that* song'.) Uses of the first sort can appear to contradict uses of the other three. For example, we somehow have to reconcile 'Velma isn't real' with 'Velma tried to escape her past'. The former is of course true. It says that nothing instantiates *being Velma*, so it clearly carries no existential import.

It seems to me that sentences like 'Velma tried to escape her past' are typically uttered from the fictional stance. So we may take them as abbreviating sentences like 'It is part of (filled-out) *Farewell, My Lovely* that some person instantiated both *being Velma* and *trying to escape one's past*'. This gives the sentence a reading that is free of the unwanted existential import.

This brings us to the matter of literary interpretation. As we all know, different notions of interpretation (some of them rather surprising) have been advocated by literary scholars and critics. No survey will be undertaken here. One common but perhaps now old-fashioned conception is that if a work has an interpretation, then it is the interpretation intended by the author. (Of course the author may not have intended any interpretation at all—'It's just a story, folks'. An author may also intend more than one interpretation, perhaps for different audiences, or to have some fun at the critics' expense.) The correct interpretation, in this sense, might not be the most plausible, interesting, or entertaining, etc. Moreover, on this notion, the interpretation goes beyond what is in the filled-out fiction. Chandler might or might not have intended Velma to symbolize a fatalistic view of life. The story is the same story whether or not he had such an intention. At the same time, a story can *suggest* a certain interpretation without its being in the filled-out fiction. It is also possible for a story to be generally taken to have an interpretation that in fact conflicts with the author's intended interpretation. And it is possible for there to be no generally accepted interpretation. The author-bound concept of interpretation clearly favors blocking existential import by invoking an operator expressing the author's intentions. Other notions of interpretation may be expected to give rise to different import-blocking operators.

The analogical uses of fictional names are quite varied and may be a bit more puzzling. But it is tempting to think that they would generally yield to analyses involving import-blocking operators. For example it seems reasonable to take 'Velma would never have sung that song' as abbreviating something like 'It is part of *Farewell, My Lovely* that Velma had certain features, and no one with those features would sing that song'.

4. Necessary Existence and Nonexistence

I have claimed on intuitive grounds that Velma's *nonexistence* is necessary. It may help to clarify this if we take a little time to consider the important and somewhat strange notion of necessary *existence*. It is of course a notion that has bedeviled many philosophers over the centuries. Twenty or so years ago it forced David Lewis to depart from his straightforward systematic deployment of possible worlds and counterparts as analyzing the boxes and diamonds. And now I need to accommodate it within the present analytic strategy.

Consider the proposition that some (given) entity, say Humphrey, exists necessarily. The natural translation is '$\exists x(Ixh \,\&\, \Box Ixe)$', with 'h' for *being Humphrey* and 'e' for the property of *existing*. It will not do for me to treat this case uniformly with typical *de re* cases by taking its truth-condition to be the entailment of e by the object-essence of the thing that in fact instantiates a. The reason is that, on intuitive actualistic and Platonic grounds, *every* property entails *existing* (including uninstantiated properties like *being a unicorn* or *being a round square* or even *not existing*). This principle is no less appealing for object-essences than for familiar general properties, for it merely reflects the very natural idea that only things that exist can be instances of properties. The challenge is thus to provide a plausible account that exploits the entailment idea even as it departs from the systematic treatment that applies successfully to overtly similar cases.

For Lewis the problem was essentially the same. His overall treatment of intuitive necessary properties was that a thing had a property necessarily iff each of its counterparts had that property in its own possible world. (That the entity-essence of the thing entails the property is the present analogue.) But of course every counterpart of Humphrey's *exists* in its own world. (Our *de re* analogue is that every entity-essence entails existing. Our *essentialist* analogue is that every person-essence (etc.) entails existing.) But neither Humphrey nor any other person or physical object exists necessarily. Lewis responded by applying the ingredients of the counterpart apparatus informally (and non-uniformly) in the special case of necessary existence. The result was that for something to exist necessarily was for it to have a counterpart in every possible world. This was certainly the right thing to say from his perspective.

Many philosophers have thought that some things 'exist necessarily' (or at least that it's an epistemic possibility that some things exist necessarily). For example, I think there really are necessary entities, specifically the Platonic properties and relations, and also that no concrete entities exist necessarily. Although I have reasons for this opinion, I will neither offer the reasons nor rely on the opinion here. What is required for an analysis of necessary existence is a perfectly general property that some entities may or may not in fact have, and which plausibly reflects our intuitive concept of necessary existence. But here it is very important to notice that this intuitive concept is in fact extremely vague. We don't really have an intuitive account of it that goes beyond restatement. (It just doesn't help to say that for something to exist necessarily is for it to be such that it could not have failed to exist. Or to say that it exists in all possible worlds, or that it exists no matter what, etc.) But this vagueness may actually make the task somewhat easier, for success then seems to depend more on overall fit with the analytic framework than on matching some reasonably clear preexisting notion.

It's also very important to appreciate that in seeking an analyzing property we are *not* seeking a property that somehow guarantees its own instantiation, one that guarantees that something *else* exists just by existing itself. Our problem is rather this. We are already *given* what exists. The question is whether, among the things that *do* exist, there is some feature that (perhaps) some of them have and others don't have, a feature that 'governs' the necessity of their (undisputed) existence. We have just seen that *having an entity-essence that entails existing* does not achieve this because it would follow that everything exists of necessity.

I believe the correct analysis is this: for a thing to exist *necessarily* is for it to have an entity-essence whose own entity-essence entails *being instantiated*. Using '$x^\wedge$' to denote the entity-essence of x (for any x), and 'i' for the property of *being instantiated*, we may capture this by saying that x exists necessarily iff $x^{\wedge\wedge}$ entails i. It is crucial to see that it doesn't follow from the fact that $x^\wedge$ entails *existing* that $x^{\wedge\wedge}$ entails i. Thus we leave room for the (epistemic) possibility that some entities x are such that $x^{\wedge\wedge}$ entails i but others are not, and this despite the fact that y entails *existing* for any entity-essence y (whether instantiated or not). Thus, if the opinion expressed above is correct, then no concrete entity x is such that $x^{\wedge\wedge}$ entails i, but every Platonic entity x is such that $x^{\wedge\wedge}$ entails i. The following diagram, with concrete entities below the line and Platonic entities above, provides a pictorial representation of this opinion by way of the Humphrey example, thereby illustrating the main idea. In the diagram single arrows represent instantiation, double arrows entailment, slashes are for negation, and 'h' denotes the person-essence, *being Humphrey*. (The diagram reflects the necessity of the property h's existence as well as the contingency of Humphrey's existence and x's existence.)

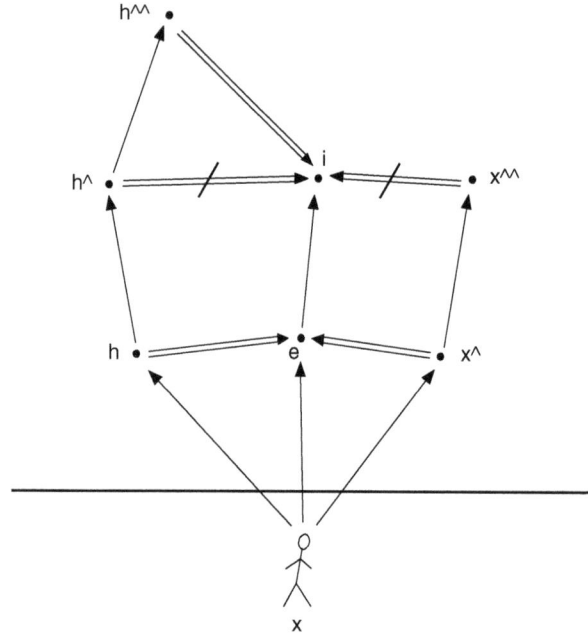

I've tried to present this proposal in a way that might forestall (or disarm in advance) a certain skeptical reaction, but I may not have succeeded. The reaction is that an arbitrary $y^{\wedge\wedge}$'s entailing i would just be the holding of a certain intrinsic relation between a pair of properties, and that surely no such state of affairs could guarantee that anything *else* exists, so that it cannot be that $y^{\wedge\wedge}$'s entailing i is what it is for y to exist necessarily.[9]

I believe this reaction is undermined by a pair of closely related problems. First, notice that it presupposes that we already have a reasonably clear intuitive concept of necessary existence, for it claims that the proposal falls short of capturing it. But I have claimed that we in fact have no such clear

[9] I thank Kirk Ludwig and Greg Ray for forcing me to deal with this question.

pre-analytic concept. I am offering a proposal to answer to what is in fact a vague and misleadingly analogical concept—the result of imagining that 'necessarily', as it modifies 'existing', somehow expresses the same basic modal notion it expresses when it modifies a more humdrum adjective like 'human'. But the concept of *existence* is already an essential component of our conception of intuitive modal properties like *being necessarily human*. This should alert us to the possibility that exactly the *same* modal qualification may not be readily applicable to the concept of existence itself, and that any felt analogy between *necessary humanness* (etc.) and *necessary existence* may just be a misleading byproduct of an accidental grammatical parallel. If something could not have existed without being human (etc.), that is far from trivial, but it's entirely trivial that nothing could have existed without existing. This suggests very strongly that *necessary humanness* and *necessary existence* are not two manifestations of a single modal phenomenon, and hence that it's no surprise if they require different analyses. So the first problem with the reaction is that it takes it that necessary existence is sufficiently clear pre-analytically for us to see that the proposal falls short of capturing it.

The second problem is this. The objection gets its rhetorical bite from the suggestion that whereas relations between properties are just inert Platonic states of affairs, the concept of necessary existence has very serious ontological heft. Thus it is made to seem absurdly magical that necessary existence should be grounded in static eternal relations between *abstracta*. Now of course it is right that nothing springs into existence as a result of intrinsic relations holding between Platonic properties. But what we're trying to capture here is the *necessity* of the existence, not the *fact* of the existence. If there are any necessary beings, then they are no different from contingent ones as far as their mere *existence* goes. For a necessary entity to exist is nothing more nor less than what it is for a contingent entity to exist.[10]

Here we are discussing things whose existence is already given, and we're asking whether, among them, there is some *further* feature that (at least potentially) sets some apart from others in a way that reflects our vague intuitive idea that their existence is somehow *necessary*. So the ontological heft is already there, presupposed in our inquiry, and we're looking for something over and above that ontological heft. I believe that when we see the matter from this perspective the objection loses its rhetorical force. The present suggestion is then that there is in fact a certain *property* that sets the necessary existents (if any) apart from the contingent ones (if any!), namely the property of having an entity-essence whose own entity-essence entails *being instantiated*.

This approach to necessary existence has what I think is a welcome companion application in the metaphysics of fiction. Earlier in this chapter I defended a conception of fiction embodying the Kripke-inspired view that the intuitive 'worlds' of works of fiction are not metaphysically possible. (Here it is best to think of the 'world' of a fiction as a complicated—but surely not *maximal*—proposition that the fiction *expresses* but doesn't *assert*.) Thus although it is possible that any logically consistent story be 'enacted' (and possible for it to be enacted by many different 'casts of characters') it is not true that the fictional names in the story denote any of the entities involved in any of the (intuitive) possible enactments (notably not in the case when it actually happens to be enacted).

On this view, a fictional name like 'Velma' does not express a person-essence that might have been instantiated. Yet in accordance with our overall Platonic picture, we still want *being Velma* (call it 'v') to entail *existing* just as any more routine

---

[10] To emphasize: to *say* of a necessary entity that it exists is to say the very same thing of it that one says of a contingent entity in saying that *it* exists.

property entails *existing*. The present suggestion is then that we may happily allow v to entail *existing* while at the same time maintaining that Velma could not have existed, simply by holding that the entity-essence of this fictional-person-essence (namely $v^\wedge$) entails *being uninstantiated*. The failure of Velma to exist is thus seen as necessary. I believe that even if one does not accept the present view about fiction, reflection on this general approach to necessary *nonexistence* helps vindicate the analysis of necessary *existence*.[11] The reason is that we don't have the distraction of an actually existing entity to mislead us. There is something about the property v that guarantees that it isn't instantiated. It's that it instantiates $v^\wedge$, and $v^\wedge$ entails *being uninstantiated*. If this is a plausible account of necessary nonexistence, then I believe the structurally parallel account of necessary existence should seem so as well.

[11] For example, those who accept 'inconsistent' properties, like *being a round square*, may hold that they entail *existing*, but that their entity-essences entail *being uninstantiated*.

7

NATURAL KIND TERMS

THE famous examples of necessary a posteriori truths offered by Saul Kripke and by Hilary Putnam are widely accepted, with reverberations across the entire landscape of analytic philosophy. They have even altered how some conceive of the enterprise of philosophy itself. But I believe the examples are incorrect. I think they are undermined by a very plausible analogue of the principle of social determination that was used in developing the present theory of names. There the idea was that the person who introduces a proper name gets to pick its *bearer*, but that its *category*—and consequently the *meaning* of the name—is determined by social use. In particular, it isn't determined by anything the name-giver says or thinks at the time of introduction, and the name generally takes hold even if what is said or thought includes serious errors about the bearer.

In the case of what we typically think of as natural kind terms—'water', 'gold', 'tiger', 'cat', and so forth—the person who introduces the term (given that there is one) gets to pick its *original extension* (the analogue of the bearer of a name), which is just whatever is ostended or described at the introduction of the term. But the *meaning* of the term (the analogue of the category of a name) is settled by subsequent social use (and relevant prior use of similar terms). Thus there is a 'division of linguistic labor', but it is somewhat different from that contemplated in Putnam (1975), where 'experts' play a key role.

Here the division is between those who introduce the term and competent users of the term in general.[1]

Roughly, here is how this works. The introducer of the term intends it to apply to all things that are of the 'same kind' as that which is in the original extension, but then users in general determine what is to count as the *same kind* by applying or refusing to apply the term both in newly encountered and counterfactually considered cases. Just as the category of 'Venus' is determined by the full range of conditions under which the name would or would not be applied, so the meaning of a term like 'water' is determined by the full range of conditions under which it would or would not be applied. In both cases the full range of conditions of application crucially includes those given in *counterfactual* use. In both cases, in an intuitive reversal of a common notion, it is the extension of the term that ultimately determines the meaning—but of course, and once again, it's the extension of the term *across the full range of possible circumstances of use.*

Thus, for example, the speech dispositions of typical users of the name 'Venus' are such that if Venus were to go out of planetary orbit, they would still apply the name. (They are disposed to give an affirmative answer to the counterfactual question, 'If Venus were to go out of orbit, would it still exist?') On the other hand, if the planet were blown to smithereens, they would not apply the name to the resulting scattered object. (They would answer negatively the counterfactual question, 'If Venus were blown to smithereens, would it still exist?') The interplay of these cases settled that the category of 'Venus' was neither *planet* nor *mereological sum*, and did so in complete independence of what the name-giver might have said or thought at the introduction.

---

[1] Putnam did hold that there generally is 'social determination' of the *extension* of a term like 'water' or 'tiger'. I will be holding that the *meaning* of such a term is socially determined.

Analogously, I believe, a situation in which the world contained XYZ as well as H_2O, and contained blends of the two, would be one in which users would unhesitatingly apply 'water' to XYZ and to blends as well as to samples of H_2O.[2] Moreover, and quite independently of the world's actual substances, early users of 'water' would have been disposed to answer affirmatively such questions as 'Might it be discovered that there are fundamentally different kinds of water?' (or '… that different samples of water have different internal structures that are invisible to the naked eye?', etc.).

As we will soon see, I believe these considerations suggest very strongly that for something to be water is *not* for it to be (liquid) H_2O, and that the meaning of 'water' is not (*liquid*) H_2O regardless of what an introducer may have said or thought (e.g., about internal structure) at the time of an introduction. Putnam conceded that the word would be used this way. He wrote, '… [I]f H_2O and *XYZ* had both been plentiful on Earth, then we would have had a case similar to the jadeite/nephrite case: it would have been correct to say that there were *two kinds of "water"*',[3] and presumably he would have thought this regardless of what was said or believed when the word was introduced. He did not, however, see this as undermining the view that 'water' is in fact a natural kind term or the notion that for something to be water is for it to be (liquid) H_2O.

Let's consider the contemporary Kripke/Putnam-inspired picture of how terms like 'water' actually work in our language, giving it as sympathetic a viewing as possible.[4] Suppose we

---

[2] Here I am thinking of XYZ—famous for its role in the 'Twin Earth' examples in Putnam (1975)—as an imaginary (but surely possible) liquid that mimics not only the superficial sensible qualities of H_2O, but also the gross functional properties like *quenching thirst*, *supporting plant growth*, and *putting out fires*. It is unclear to me whether this notion, with its emphasis on functional properties, is exactly the same as Putnam's.

[3] See *Mind, Language and Reality: Philosophical Papers*, ii: 241.

[4] I say 'contemporary Kripke/Putnam-inspired picture' because neither of them has put the matter in quite these terms. I do, however, think this is how they are commonly understood.

came upon convincing evidence that the word 'water' was introduced by an early English speaker, who uttered a Very Old English variant of the sentence, 'Let the term "water" apply to any liquid that has the same underlying internal structure that the stuff that is now before us in fact has, whatever that structure might be like in detail'. And suppose also that the stuff in question was in fact liquid H_2O. Finally, suppose that the Very Old English precursor of 'water' was not similar to any term in any other language familiar to those who spoke Very Old English, so that it wouldn't be arguable that this was just an adoption of an extramural variant of a previously introduced term. Then I think it is fair to say that this picture—again, I believe, now the orthodox view—is one according to which natural kind terms work *as if* they had been introduced in this highly idealized way, and that this (together with the fact that the sample was H_2O) establishes *that water is H_2O*.[5] From this it is typically concluded that the *meaning* of 'water' is (*liquid*) H_2O.[6] The sentence 'Water is H_2O', taken as expressing the identity of the property of *being water* with the property of *being H_2O*, would then express a proposition that was necessarily true but, as it was claimed, a posteriori. The proposition was held to be necessary because it is expressed by an 'identity sentence' whose terms are (or could readily be replaced by) 'rigid designators'. It was claimed to be a posteriori because it was held that empirical investigation is obviously required to establish its truth.

Let us set aside worries about whether it is appropriate to view this sentence as an 'identity sentence' and also worries about 'rigid designators'. We'll just accept that the claim of

---

[5] Kripke, speaking of 'gold', admits that contemplating a hypothetical baptism of the substance is somewhat artificial. See Kripke (1972, 1980: 135). He is not committed to any claim to the effect that such a baptism actually occurred for any natural kind term.

[6] Putnam's view is a bit more intricate. For present purposes we need not delve into the subtleties. See Putnam (1975).

property identity, if true, is necessary. There remains something quite odd about how the two claims fit together. The claim of necessity depends on understanding the sentence as expressing a 'property identity'.[7] But the empirical investigation does not seem directed at a question of putative property identity *at all*. It is directed at discovering the internal structure of a specific sample of stuff in fact deemed to be *water*. The proposition most obviously verified empirically would simply be the proposition that *such and such stuff* was H_2O. This is surely a posteriori but it isn't at all clear that it's necessary. Indeed, on the present account of physical objects, very small parts of that stuff might have been arranged in such a way that we would have the same stuff but it wouldn't be H_2O. It is fair to say that such an investigation also would have verified that some stuff that was in fact taken by some competent speakers to be *water*, and which hence was likely to be superficially similar to the originally ostended stuff, was H_2O. Charitably, we might say further that it would have been empirically verified that some stuff that superficially resembled the stuff of a long-gone sample was H_2O. But it is entirely implausible that such a proposition would be a necessary truth. Further, to infer the *property identity* from the investigation certainly requires further contingent premises, involving uninvestigated samples, as we will mention again below.

Thus I think there are serious and immediate problems with the orthodox view. But, as I see it, the most fundamental problem (and one related to these) is that no such idealized introduction would provide an epistemically sound basis for subsequent use of the term, since for centuries no one would be in a position to know that stuff similar in appearance and function had the same underlying internal structure as the stuff

---

[7] Of course, as is well known and has been endlessly discussed, the same proposition is *arguably* expressed by 'Water is water', and that proposition is evidently not a posteriori. But let this go.

that was present at the introduction.[8] For centuries, people would only be in a position to request a glass of stuff that *might* be water, or that was *like* water. They would, literally, not know the meaning of the term. I find this sharply counterintuitive. It is much more plausible, I believe, to think that people really were able to use 'water' with reasonable confidence and authority *even given the imagined details of the introduction*. Just as in the case of proper names, I think the details of any description used at the imagined introduction are incidental to the meaning of the term.

Here is a second problem. Although in the idealization the stuff at the introduction was H_2O, surely it might have been a blend of H_2O and XYZ as recently imagined. If so, then the stuff confronting the imagined introducer of the term would not have had a single underlying structure in any reasonable sense of that term. So the embedded description would go unsatisfied and, taking things at face value, the term would not have been successfully introduced. I find this indefensible in view of the fact that 'water' would have been used ubiquitously and with seeming success for centuries thereafter. Eventually it would have been discovered that there were two fundamental kinds of water, and that the water one encounters on Earth is generally a mixture of the two kinds, but that either kind could crop up in isolation or in a laboratory. Just as we saw in the 'Venus'/star case, the description invoked at the introduction can be *dead wrong* without affecting the success of the introduction.[9]

---

[8] Putnam (*Mind, Language and Reality*, ii: 241) concedes that '... we could have been in the same epistemological situation with respect to a liquid with no hidden structure as we were actually with respect to water at one time', but he does not see this as bearing so heavily on the actual meaning of the term as I do.

[9] Putnam's concession (see fn. 3 above) that in these circumstances there would have been two kinds of water makes his overall view effectively *disjunctive*: either the actual substance (etc.) has a single underlying structure and we have a natural kind term, or else it doesn't and the meaning of the term is given by a more superficial conjunction or the like. This again has the counterintuitive

A third problem arises from another XYZ case. Suppose the stuff at the introduction was actually H_2O, but that H_2O was in fact extremely rare and XYZ, on the other hand, was common. The imagined introducer of 'water', of course, wouldn't know about these details. A literal understanding of the undiluted orthodox view yields the conclusion that although the term would have been successfully introduced, nearly all subsequent uses of it would be incorrect because they would be directed upon stuff that was actually XYZ (or blends). I believe this conclusion is too fantastic to be believed. It seems to me that when people in the imagined circumstances apply 'water' to stuff that is actually XYZ, they are speaking perfectly good English, and they are getting it right. The term, *even if introduced as imagined*, applies correctly to either substance and to blends. It would also apply to any other substance indistinguishable from these in superficial appearance and function. It should have the same meaning regardless of whether H_2O or XYZ (etc.) was ostended at the introduction and also regardless of what similar substances are to be found elsewhere in the world. The intuitive general principle here is that any *ordinary* term in well-established use would have had the same meaning had it been established in *different* circumstances as long as they were no different *epistemically* for the users of the term. This is the backbone of the present version of social determination, according to which the meaning of a term is settled by how it is used.

There are various ways one might dilute the orthodox view so as to accommodate social determination. One idea would have the meaning of a term reflect social use *together with* contingent facts about which substances lie in the socially determined extension—a kind of 'social externalism'. In the original case, where we assume there is nothing like XYZ to

---

consequence that seemingly competent early users of such terms literally don't know what they mean.

muddy the waters, the term would mean (*liquid*) H_2O, as in the orthodox picture. But in the second case, where there is a mixture, we might (charitably?) understand the introductory proclamation as yielding something like *H_2O or XYZ or a mixture* as the meaning.[10]

Kripke, speaking of gold, reveals a certain *ex post facto* or retroactive susceptibility to a diluted approach, but for him I believe it is a very awkward accommodation. He says, 'If, on the other hand, the supposition that there is one uniform substance or kind in the original sample proves more radically in error, reactions can vary: *sometimes we may declare that there are two kinds of gold*, sometimes we may drop the term "gold". (These possibilities are not supposed to be exhaustive.)' (136, my emphasis). And Putnam says, '[I]f there is a hidden structure, then generally it determines what it is to be a member of the natural kind, not only in the actual world, but in all possible worlds... But the local water, or whatever, may have two or more hidden structures—or so many that "hidden structure" becomes irrelevant, and superficial characteristics become the decisive ones.' (*Mind, Language and Reality*, ii: 241.)

So, in this case, the meaning of 'gold' would have been something other than *Au*, something disjunctive or dispositional or the like—neither Kripke nor Putnam offers details. Nor do they say whether in such a circumstance 'gold' (etc.) would have had this meaning all along or whether it would acquire it only when the facts were in. But if the latter, then we would still need to know what it meant originally, and neither *Au* nor *AUX*[11] is a plausible candidate. Thus it seems we must choose between following the literal line, with the result that the term

---

[10] Or perhaps: *any substance indistinguishable from H_2O and XYZ in sensory and functional properties or mixtures of such substances*, in order to accommodate multiple H_2O-ringer cases.

[11] Here I mimic 'XYZ': AUX is intended to be a perfect sensory and functional ringer for Au. (I note that 'XAU' is already taken—it's the ISO currency code for Au.)

did not have a meaning until it was discovered that there are two kinds of gold, or else holding that it had the disjunctive or dispositional (etc.) meaning all along.

This is not a happy choice. The first option makes it hard to understand how scientists could have discovered that there were two kinds of gold in the first place since the term would have had no meaning at the time. They would, after all, be identifying some stuff as gold *first*, and only *then* subjecting it to scientific analysis. They and everyone else would have been speaking of gold well in advance and seemingly would have been making good sense. The second option would be one or another diluted approach involving both social determination and contingent facts, as discussed above. This is likely the most reasonable interpretation of Kripke and Putnam, but it too raises a difficult problem.

The problem is that we would have a radical asymmetry between genuine natural kind cases and *faux* natural kind cases. But both kinds of cases have something very important in common, for (almost always) the early users of the term simply don't know whether they're dealing with a genuine natural kind. (Indeed, they may not even have the *concept* of a natural kind.) So why should we not think that the meaning of the term (at least at that point) reflects no stand at all on this question? More crisply, why should the meaning reflect a mere supposition in one kind of case but not in the other? In the *faux* cases there is no less reason to think there would be such a supposition. In fact it doesn't seem very plausible to me that early users of such terms really held (even tacitly) a *natural kind* supposition in the first place. More plausible, I think, is the idea that the early users were simply interested in having or avoiding stuff and things with certain external appearances and observable functional features. ('We need to get more of this (kind of) stuff.' 'Watch out for these (sorts of) things.' Etc.) I believe the undeniable fact that they would have *called* XYZ 'water' and AUX 'gold', etc., bears this out.

We may further this perspective by considering the term 'air' (and perhaps also, completing an ancient quartet, 'earth' and 'fire').[12] What reason could be given for thinking that the treatment of 'water' would not also apply to 'air'? Air, of course, is neither an element nor a compound like H_2O, but rather a mixture of an indefinite variety of compounds and elements, and these ingredients may be present in widely varying proportions. So if we apply the undiluted orthodox view, the outcome is that there simply isn't much air at all and hence that most everyday uses of the term are incorrect. That cannot be right. Are we to believe that the introducer of the term (if there was one) was onto the idea that there is no such single substance as pure air, whereas the introducer of 'water' had some fairly clear notion that there was such a single substance as pure water? The initial senses of 'water' and 'air' should be parallel. Either both are natural kind terms or neither is, and I believe the present thinking gives the edge to the latter appraisal.[13]

So far I've been preaching the social determination gospel with the aid of thought experiments about how terms like 'water' would be used in different possible circumstances. This is of course the same strategy that was very effectively used by Kripke in his advocacy of what became the orthodox view. It is easy to find oneself nodding in approval (as well as smiling in appreciation) when reading the relevant passages in *Naming and Necessity*. How can we come to such different conclusions? What's really going on here? Let's look in some detail.

Beginning on page 116, Kripke turns his attention from individual entities (and their essential properties) to substances and natural kinds. He will attempt to convince us that terms for substances and natural kinds behave very much as he has just

---

[12] Greg Fitch suggested air and urged me to emphasize it. (Despite this, I believe he continued to favor a Kripke/Putnam-inspired position.)

[13] Or we might even consider liberalizing our concept of natural kind. What, after all, is more natural than air? I won't pursue this.

argued proper names behave.[14] The first example he discusses in detail is *gold* and Kant's contention that it is part of the concept of gold that it is a yellow metal. Kripke quickly sets aside the question of whether it is part of the concept of gold that it is a *metal* (pleading inadequate knowledge of the chemistry of metals) and turns to the question of whether *yellowness* is part of the concept. He offers a thought experiment to show that we could discover that gold in fact is not yellow, but rather blue. It is actually a parallel, two-phase thought experiment, not very convincing as actually stated, but easily improved. One phase involves the imagined prevalence of illusions in areas where we find gold mines. (But what about the gold in Tiffany's?!) The other imagines a demon corrupting the vision of those entering the mines. (Again, what about the uncorrupted (?) vision of those entering Tiffany's?)

The key idea is of course simply that there might be something special going on that makes gold appear yellow though it is actually blue, but in one part of the thought experiment the something special is a natural phenomenon, while in the other it isn't. To make the experiment more convincing we need to make the something special take hold *wherever there is gold*, and there are various ways this might be done. Here are three: (1) Imagine that all gold generates a surrounding 'aura' which modifies the wavelength of light just after it is reflected. (2) Imagine that by sheer coincidence gold has so far always been located in micro-atmospheres that generate illusions of the sort Kripke imagined. (3) Imagine that God (or a powerful demon) modifies our vision whenever we look at gold. In variation (1) we would need to be able to detect the aura and, in effect, neutralize it in order to arrive at the conclusion that gold is actually blue. A similar comment applies in variation (2). Whereas these cases involve far-fetched natural possibilities, variation (3) is more akin to a skeptical hypothesis, and it would

---

[14] Of course they function very similarly on the present account too!

be trickier, but not impossible, to arrive at the conclusion that gold is actually blue. (1) and (3) indeed are cases in which it would be natural to say that gold was not yellow. But they are also cases in which we surely would say that gold *appears yellow*. In case (2) there is some temptation to say that gold appears yellow, or at least has appeared yellow, but when the massive coincidence unravels, we will surely change our minds. Kripke concludes the dual thought experiment as follows:

> Would there on this basis be an announcement in the newspapers: 'It has turned out that there is no gold. Gold does not exist. What we took to be gold is not in fact gold.'? It seems to me that there would be no such announcement. On the contrary, what would be announced would be that though it appeared that gold was yellow, in fact gold has turned out not to be yellow, but blue. The reason is, I think, that we use 'gold' as a term for a certain *kind* of thing. Others have discovered this kind of thing and we have heard of it.... The kind of thing is *thought* to have certain identifying marks.... We might discover that we are wrong about them. Further, there might be a substance which has all the identifying marks ... but which is not the same kind of thing, which is not the same substance.... Such a thing is, for example, as we well know, iron pyrites or fool's gold. This is not another kind of gold. (118–19)

Taken superficially this may seem convincing, but Kripke will go on to reveal, in effect, that he is taking 'kind' to be synonymous with 'natural kind', and it is here that I part company. I believe we indeed used 'gold' as a term for a certain *kind* of thing, but that the kind was determined by how it was *in fact* used (and moreover that it was used in a way that ruled out pyrite). I also think that, at least prior to the atomic theory, it was not used as a natural kind term even if all of the stuff to which it was actually applied fell under a natural kind. Without explicitly saying so, Kripke is at pains to undermine the idea that 'gold' expresses a conjunction of superficial appearance properties like *being yellow*. If *being yellow* isn't part of the concept, then we should not expect that any other similar superficial property will be essential to gold, so that the meaning of the term will not be some conjunction of such properties.

I agree that 'gold' does not express a conjunction of superficial appearance properties. Despite this, it's worth noting that a savvy observer *can* tell gold from fool's gold just by sensory inspection.[15] It isn't called 'fool's gold' for nothing. No doubt there have been fools, so the term 'gold' *has* been misapplied, but surely people were distinguishing gold from fool's gold (and not regarding fool's gold as a different kind of gold) long before they knew about the atomic structure of gold and the molecular structure of pyrite. For example, the two substances have dramatically different melting points.[16] An early goldsmith, working with gold and pyrite, and thinking at first that the latter was gold, would soon discover this fact along with gross differences in malleability, etc., and would conclude that pyrite wasn't gold. We indeed intend 'gold' to apply to a certain *kind* of thing, and that a similar looking substance should have such dramatic differences would be conclusive evidence that it wasn't the same kind of thing. But it simply doesn't follow that the kind in question is *the element with atomic number 79*.

Kripke would insist that it was a subsequent empirical discovery that gold is the element with atomic number 79. I would say that after certain *samples of gold* were experimentally determined to have atomic number 79, it was *hypothesized* that *all gold* has this atomic structure, and that this is something that *in fact* may not be true. All it would take to make it false would be the discovery of a substance whose superficial appearance and functional properties were the same as the element's, but without being that element. If this were to occur, the announcement in the newspapers *would* be that there are

---

[15] For example, they have different shades of yellow. There are normally also perceptible shape differences in naturally occurring samples. Further, when rubbed with hard objects, gold gives off no odor, but pyrite smells sulfurous.

[16] About 1064°C for gold and 2140°C for pyrites. They also are differentiated by simple hardness and malleability tests that require no special equipment.

two kinds of gold. It would then be discovered that some of the gold in the great jewelry collections was not elemental gold, or was a blend of two or more varieties of gold. The gold industry would proceed unruffled and no one would care whether the gold in an ingot or a wedding ring was Au or AUX, or a combination of the two.

The fact that the activities of demons (or weird local atmospheric conditions) might make us wrong about some, or even all, of the sensible and functional properties of gold does not threaten the conclusion that if we are right about these characteristics, then to be gold is to be a substance having these very characteristics, for it is to substances having these characteristics that 'gold' would have been applied in subsequent social use.[17] If we're wrong about a few of them, then a revision can take place. We thought gold was yellow, but it's actually a *blue* metal, which often or even always appears yellow, and with such and such melting point, ductility, malleability, and the like. If we're wrong about them all, then the term expresses a conjunction of the *actual* properties of the corresponding types that we've somehow been systematically misled about, and we could ultimately discover this. What we could not discover is that it's essential to gold that it's an element and that it has atomic number 79.

Indeed, if a demon could confuse us so thoroughly that we thought gold was yellow when it was actually blue, why could it not similarly confuse us into thinking that gold is an element with atomic number 79? Arriving at the empirical conclusion that a sample of gold is such an element after all requires certain sorts of human perceptions, so all the demon has to do is to distort them. Perhaps the entire periodic table is shifted with respect to atomic number as a consequence of demonic activity, and the correct number for Au is really 80. It

---

[17] We could, of course, hedge by saying that to be gold is to be something that *appears* thus and so, *appears* to function in such and such ways, etc.

thus seems that the demon thought experiment applies equally in the cases of atomic number and color, and a complication of the atmospheric illusion phase of the thought experiment should as well.

Kripke himself acknowledges this a bit later, after discussing tigers. He asks, 'Is it a necessary or a contingent property of gold that it has the atomic number 79? Certainly we could find out that we were mistaken .... Certainly we didn't know it from time immemorial. So in that sense, gold could turn out not to have atomic number 79.' (123) So if the earlier thought experiment is taken to show that it isn't part of the concept of gold that it is *yellow*, then the same should be said of its *having atomic number 79*. But now Kripke asks, 'Given that gold *does* have the atomic number 79, could something be gold without having the atomic number 79?' He will arrive at a negative conclusion in a somewhat circuitous way. He continues, 'Let us suppose the scientists have investigated the nature of gold and have found that it is part of the very nature of this substance, so to speak, that it have the atomic number 79.' (124)

There ensues a confusing discussion in which iron pyrites sometimes appears to be the subject, but other times seems merely to be a surrogate for arbitrary gold-imitating substances, including those that would be dead ringers, for example the imagined AUX. I have already conceded that Kripke is right that pyrite isn't a form of gold, but I also claimed that this could easily have been concluded (and probably was) before the atomic theory of matter was available. Next, after the distraction of pyrite, Kripke says, 'Given that gold *is* this element [i.e., the one with atomic number 79–MJ], any other substance ... would not be gold .... So if this consideration is right, it tends to show that such statements representing scientific discoveries about what this stuff *is* are not contingent truths but necessary truths in the strictest possible sense.' (125) And a moment later he adds, 'In particular, then, present scientific theory is such that it is part of the nature of gold as we have it to be an element with atomic number 79. It will therefore be necessary and not contingent that gold be an element with atomic number 79.' (125)

What shall we make of all this? I believe that when Kripke says, 'Given that gold *is* this element, any other substance...would not be gold', he is begging the question of the meaning of 'gold' (and hence the question of the necessary properties of *gold*—the properties that *being gold* entails). For if, as I have suggested, 'gold' would have applied correctly to substances with a different internal structure, for example to (the imaginary) AUX, then the fact (if it is a fact) that all of the actual gold is composed of atoms with atomic number 79 does not ensure that it is necessary that gold is such an element. This broader conception of 'gold' (and gold) cannot reasonably be ruled out a priori. But that is exactly what Kripke is doing here.

Basing the claim that gold is the element with atomic number 79 on a few empirical tests conducted on what had to be miniscule quantities of the world's gold supply is certainly at least rash. Presumably, the scientists who did the empirical tests first identified some samples as *gold*, and *then* performed tests that revealed (skeptical hypotheses aside) that these were samples of an element with atomic number 79. It obviously doesn't follow that every sample in the world that would *at the time* have been identified as a sample of *gold* would consist of atoms having atomic number 79. That is a flamboyant inductive projection (even if true). Clearly, if AUX had fallen into the hands of the testing scientists instead of Au, it would have been accepted as a sample of gold, and the testing would have revealed an internal structure dramatically different from that of Au.

How were these scientists able to identify something as a sample of gold in the first place? I believe the answer can only be that it possessed all of the superficial appearance *and* routine functional features that were taken at the time to characterize gold. In other words, the sample would fall correctly into the socially determined extension of 'gold'. By the time of the early atomic theory, this extension would most likely have excluded iron pyrites (for example because of its high melting point). But it would *not* have excluded the imaginary AUX had such existed. Kripke claims (124) that pyrite has many of the properties by which we *originally* identified gold and acknowledges that further properties were added to these over time, presumably properties that excluded pyrite if the totality of the original properties did not. On this picture we start out with some 'identifying marks' (some of which may actually be incorrect) and then we learn more and add to the possibly corrected original list.

But of course there really is no list. There is instead just the collective informed use of the term, which at a given time may not count something as 'gold' that it once did. (Such a thing may indeed be iron pyrites—no one can really know.) What we do know, however, is that prior to the atomic theory, gold could not have been identified by a collection of properties that entailed that it had atomic number 79. So there might have been a substance that would have been identified as gold even by the most sophisticated chemists of the time, but which would not have been the element Au.

A conspicuous and I believe crucial problem in Kripke's discussion is his emphasis on external appearances at the expense of observable functional properties.[18] This makes it easy to conclude that there could be fool's water, fool's tigers, and the like, and that these would not be different kinds of water or tigers, etc. But it also makes it *too* easy to conclude that to be water, etc., is to possess a certain very specific internal structure. He has, in effect, set up a false dichotomy: either

---

[18] Thus he imagines animals that look just like tigers but are in fact very peculiar reptiles, and supposes that the difference is a matter of internal structure (or species). (120) But are we supposed to imagine these creatures crawling about on their bellies or moving like regular tigers? Questions like this obviously have a great deal to do with whether we might wind up thinking there are two kinds of tigers.

these terms express (conjunctions of) external appearances (the 'identifying marks') or else they express internal structural features. But neither choice conforms to how these terms would actually have been used in situations like those we have considered here. On the social determination conception the truth lies somewhere in between, with functional properties playing a critical role. As a crude generalization, if two (or more) internally divergent types of creatures had been called, say, *tigers*, then there would have been two different kinds of tigers and the term would not have been a species-term. The same goes for substances and terms like 'air', 'water', and 'gold'. Such terms would simply have expressed intuitive conjunctions of appearance and functional properties. But all along we have actually been in a situation epistemically indistinguishable from the ones we have considered here, so that such terms have not been species-terms for us either, regardless of whether there is a single underlying structure (water?) or not (air).

That leaves us with the question of what happened, say, to 'gold' when the scientists determined that their samples had atomic number 79. One thing that surely did not happen was the discovery of a new identifying mark of *gold*. Miners, goldsmiths, jewelers, and mints were not thereby given a new and routine way to test for this property, nor do we have such a test now. So 'gold' would have continued to be applied to samples—which might or might not be Au—on the very basis upon which the scientists selected their samples for testing in the first place. There may now also be some routine tests for *gold* that were not known during the early days of the atomic theory. But passing such a test (even setting aside skepticism about results, etc.) would not entail that a sample was Au.

Despite all of this, it is undeniable that there is *now* a sense in which 'gold' *means* Au—a sense in which the word expresses the property of *being Au*, that is, *being the element with atomic number 79*. Should we view this as a newer and technical sense of the term, standing alongside the evolved nontechnical sense, or as a further but deep-going revision of what was previously just an evolving appearance/function sense? This is a distinction without *much* of a difference because either way we now have a sense that is technical because it goes beyond readily observable features and reflects a scientific theory of the internal structures of things. The only difference is whether a nontechnical, appearance/function sense survives the new discovery.

I favor the view that the nontechnical sense survives, and that we now have a new sense with an accompanying empirical hypothesis. The hypothesis is that there is a *single* underlying structure that makes something be *gold* (in the nontechnical sense). Such a hypothesis of course might or might not be correct, but if it proves incorrect, a consequence will be that there are two (or more) kinds of nontechnical gold, that only one of them is technical gold, and that either another technical sense or else another technical term altogether will emerge. But if we reject this in favor of an evolved and *now* technical sense, then we might later discover AUX and conclude that it's not gold (in this evolved and newly technical sense).

I see no room here for necessity a posteriori. In the nontechnical sense 'Gold is Au', understood as making a claim about the world's gold supply and not as a 'property identity', expresses a contingent a posteriori truth (if it expresses a true proposition in the first place). Understood as a property identity it is of course false. In the new technical sense, it expresses a property identity that is both necessary and a priori. In the evolved technical sense, it would again express a necessary a priori truth. I find no a posteriori necessity lurking in this neighborhood. So I believe it is fair to say that the Kripke/Putnam examples depend on a mistaken idealization of the workings of natural language.

A slightly different sort of case, not featuring a putative property identity claim, might help motivate this a bit further. Suppose that when people started using 'air', they were aware of the fact that we need to breathe it in order to survive. This would have been its most important functional property.

Suppose also that they knew that there were deadly gases and they said things like, 'Don't go in that cave—it has no air!', when they knew a deadly gas filled the cave. They would refuse to apply 'air' except to gases that were breathable without imminent danger. Later it would be discovered that air contains about 21 percent oxygen in the form O_2, and that it's the O_2 in air that keeps our bodies going. This might be taken as an empirical discovery of an *essential* feature of air. Then the proposition *that air contains O_2* would be a candidate for a necessary a posteriori truth, but one that was not even arguably a property identity.

I don't think it matters that we're not dealing directly with a potential property identity. In our story, which is plausibly the actual course of events, it would be true that there might have been another gas, say XOX (like 'XYZ') that was a sensory and functional ringer for O_2, so that our lungs could process it with the same salubrious effect as O_2. Parts of the world might have had atmospheres of which 21 percent was XOX and without O_2. There can be no real question but that people would have applied the term 'air' to this gas. So, according to the present way of thinking, it would be socially determined that 'air' did not express a property that a gas could instantiate only if it contained O_2. It would instead express an intuitive conjunction of superficial appearance and observable functional properties. The hypothesized 'XAIR' would instantiate this property without having to contain any O_2. The empirical finding that air contains O_2 (if true) would be *contingent a posteriori*. Thus it would parallel the empirical finding that the world's gold is Au or that the world's water is H_2O.

REFERENCES

Adams, Robert Merrihew (1981), 'Actualism and Thisness', *Synthèse*, 49: 3–41.
—— (1974), 'Theories of Actuality', *Noûs* 8: 211–31.
Baker, Lynne Rudder (2000), *Persons and Bodies* (Cambridge: Cambridge University Press).
—— (1997), 'Why Constitution is not Identity', *Journal of Philosophy*, 94: 599–621.
Bealer, George (2004), 'An Inconsistency in Direct Reference Theory', *Journal of Philosophy*, 101: 574–93.
—— (1982), *Quality and Concept* (Oxford: Oxford University Press).
Black, Max (1952), 'The Identity of Indiscernibles', *Mind*, 61: 153–64.
Boolos, George (1984), 'To Be is to Be the Value of a Variable (or to Be some Values of some Variables)', *Journal of Philosophy*, 81: 430–49.
Burge, Tyler (1973), 'Reference and Proper Names', *Journal of Philosophy*, 70: 425–39.
Carnap, Rudolf (1947), *Meaning and Necessity* (Chicago: University of Chicago Press).
Chandler, Raymond (1940), *Farewell, My Lovely* (New York: Ballantine Books).
Chihara, Charles S. (1998), *The Worlds of Possibility* (Oxford: Oxford University Press).
Graff, Delia (now Fara, Delia Graff) (2001), 'Descriptions as Predicates', *Philosophical Studies*, 102: 1–42.
Grim, Patrick (1984), 'There is no Set of all Truths', *Analysis*, 44: 206–8.
Heller, Mark (1990), *The Ontology of Physical Objects: Four Dimensional Hunks of Matter* (Cambridge: Cambridge University Press).
Hintikka, Jaakko (1961), 'Modality and Quantification', *Theoria*, 27: 119–28.
Hirsch, Eli (1982), *The Concept of Identity* (Oxford: Oxford University Press).

Jubien, Michael (2007), 'Analyzing Modality', *Oxford Studies in Metaphysics*, 3: 99–139.
—— (2004), 'On Quine's Rejection of Intensional Entities', *Midwest Studies in Philosophy*, 28 (*The American Philosophers*): 209–25.
—— (2001a), 'Thinking about Things', *Philosophical Perspectives*, 15 (*Metaphysics*): 1–15.
—— (2001b), 'Propositions and the Objects of Thought', *Philosophical Studies*, 104: 47–62.
—— (1997), *Contemporary Metaphysics: An Introduction* (Oxford: Blackwell Publishers).
—— (1996), 'The Myth of Identity Conditions', in *Philosophical Perspectives*, 10 (*Metaphysics*): 344–56.
—— (1993), *Ontology, Modality, and the Fallacy of Reference* (Cambridge: Cambridge University Press).
—— (1988), 'Problems with Possible Worlds', in D. F. Austin (ed.), *Philosophical Analysis* (Dordrecht: Kluwer Academic Publishers), 299–322.
Katz, Jerrold J. (1990), *The Metaphysics of Meaning* (Cambridge, Mass.: MIT Press).
King, Jeffrey C. (2007), *The Nature and Structure of Content* (Oxford: Oxford University Press).
Kripke, Saul A. (1972, 1980), *Naming and Necessity* (Cambridge, Mass.: Harvard University Press).
—— (1963), 'Semantical Considerations on Modal Logic', *Acta Philosophica Fennica*, 16: 83–94, repr. in Linsky (1971: 63–72).
Lewis, David (1991), *Parts of Classes* (Oxford: Basil Blackwell).
—— (1986), *On the Plurality of Worlds* (Oxford: Basil Blackwell).
—— (1983), *Philosophical Papers*, i (Oxford: Oxford University Press).
—— (1978), 'Truth in Fiction', *American Philosophical Quarterly*, 15: 37–46, repr. with postscripts, in Lewis (1983: 261–80).
—— (1973), *Counterfactuals* (Cambridge, Mass.: Harvard University Press).
—— (1968), 'Counterpart Theory and Quantified Modal Logic', *Journal of Philosophy*, 65: 113–26.
Linsky, Leonard (ed.) (1971), *Reference and Modality* (Oxford: Oxford University Press).
Lockwood, Michael (1975), 'On Predicating Proper Names', *Philosophical Review*, 84: 471–98.

References

Marcus, Ruth Barcan (1993), *Modalities* (Oxford: Oxford University Press).

McTaggart, J. M. E. (1927), *The Nature of Existence*, ii (Cambridge: Cambridge University Press).

Merricks, Trenton (1999), 'Persistence, Parts, and Presentism', *Noûs*, 33: 421–38.

—— (1995), 'On the Incompatibility of Enduring and Perduring Entities', *Mind*, 104: 523–31.

Montague, Richard (1974), *Formal Philosophy: Selected Papers*, ed. Richmond H. Thomason (New Haven: Yale University Press).

Plantinga, Alvin (1974), *The Nature of Necessity* (Oxford: Oxford University Press).

Putnam, Hilary (1975), 'The Meaning of "Meaning"', *Minnesota Studies in the Philosophy of Science*, vii (*Language, Mind and Knowledge*), repr. in Hilary Putnam, *Mind, Language and Reality: Philosophical Papers*, ii (Cambridge: Cambridge University Press, 1975), 215–71.

Quine, W. V. O. (1969), *Ontological Relativity and Other Essays* (New York: Columbia University Press).

—— (1960), *Word and Object* (Cambridge, Mass.: MIT Press).

—— (1953, 1961, 1980), *From a Logical Point of View*. (Cambridge: Harvard University Press).

Roy, Tony (1995), 'In Defense of Linguistic Ersatzism', *Philosophical Studies*, 80: 217–42.

Russell, Bertrand (1905), 'On Denoting', in Bertrand Russell, *Logic and Knowledge: Essays 1901–1950*, ed. Robert C. Marsh, 1956 (London: George Allen & Unwin, Ltd., and New York: The Macmillan Company).

Shalkowski, S. A. (1994), 'The Ontological Ground of the Alethic Modality', *Philosophical Review*, 103: 669–88.

Sider, Theodore (2003), 'Reductive Theories of Modality', in Michael J. Loux and Dean W. Zimmerman (eds.), *The Oxford Handbook of Metaphysics*, 2003 (Oxford: Oxford University Press).

—— (2001), *Four-Dimensionalism: An Ontology of Persistence and Time* (Oxford: Oxford University Press).

Sommers, Fred (1969), 'Do We Need Identity?', *Journal of Philosophy* 66: 499–504.

Stalnaker, Robert (1976), 'Possible Worlds', *Noûs*, 10: 65–75.

References

Tichý, Pavel (1987), 'Individuals and their Roles', in Tichý (2005: 711–48).
—— (1988), *The Foundations of Frege's Logic* (Berlin: de Gruyter).
—— (2005), *Pavel Tichý's Collected Papers in Logic and Philosophy*, eds. V. Svoboda, B. Jespersen, C. Cheyne (Dunedin, N. Z.: University of Otago Press).
Van Inwagen, Peter (1994), 'Composition as Identity', *Philosophical Perspectives*, 8 (*Logic and Language*): 207–20.
—— (1990a), 'Four-Dimensional Objects', *Noûs*, 24: 245–55.
—— (1990b), *Material Beings* (Ithaca, N. Y.: Cornell University Press).
—— (1987), 'When are Objects Parts?', *Philosophical Perspectives*, 1 (*Metaphysics*): 21–47.
—— (1986), 'Two Concepts of Possible Worlds', *Midwest Studies in Philosophy*, 11 (*Studies in Essentialism*): 185–213.
Walton, Kendall L. (1978), 'Fearing Fictions', *Journal of Philosophy*, 75: 5–27.

INDEX

'aboutness' 127, 132
abstract entities
  assumptions about properties
    and 54–7
  direct reference and 139–40
  entity-essences and 89
  face value argument and 41–3
  identity conditions and 46–54
  theoretical posits and 43–6
  world theory and 78–82
abstract worlds 78–82
abundance 54–5
actualism
  modal semantics and 71–2, 73–4
  property entailment and 100
actuality, concept of 124–6
analogical uses of names 170–1
application dispositions 134–5, 136, 138, 142–3, 146–9, 180–1
artifacts
  categories and 147 n.
  DR theories and 115–18
attributes, *see* properties

Bealer, George 121 n.
bearer, of a name 123
being a person
  controversial entailments
    of 155–6
  essentialism and 104–7
being a physical object
  as fundamental category 86–8
  as relational property 4–9
being x, property of 89
Black, Max 32
Boolos, George 5 n.
Burge, Tyler 154 n.

Carnap, Rudolf 51–2, 53
Carroll, Lewis 48
cases and examples, *see* thought
  experiments
category, *see also* meaning
  being a physical object as 87–8
  drift and 143–5
  of a name 135–8, 141–9
  property-based strategy and 135
  social determination of 136–8
  unclear cases and 138, 141–9
causal chain view 122–3
Chandler, Raymond 164–71
Chihara, Charles S. 73 n.
class, concept of, 49–51
'coincident objects' 129 n.
combinations 3–4
compatibility relation
  as 'dual' notion with
    entailment 94
  essentialist thought experiments
    and 106–7
  formal expression of 131
  possibility and 94, 131
composition 2–4, 6, *see also*
  objectification
conceptual reduction 95–100
concrete entities, *see also* direct
  reference (DR) theories;
  ordinary names; physical
  objects; physical reality
  'barn' example 10–11, 12 n., 14
  Black's globes and 32
  'clay/statue' example and 16–17, 19, 20
  concept of matter and 1–2
  as constituents of
    propositions 151 n.

concrete entities, (*cont.*)
Dali museum example 17 n.
'dog' example 37–8
great divide and 15–22
identities of objects and 22–36
mereological essentialism
and 36–40
necessary existence and 172
'olive-sized object'
example 19–20
persistence through time
and 9–15
quantification and 2–9
'Ship of Theseus' story
and 16–17, 18, 21–2
'two-piece suits' example 3–4
context, and use of name 149, 153–5
contingent relations
category and 144–5
necessity in world theory
and 74–6
convention Q 7–9, *see also*
Q-objects
entity-essences and 88–9
mereological essentialism
and 38–40
object identity ('QPO')
and 23–32, 34–6
with perdurance ('QP') 12–15, 22–3, 34
single-quantifier approach
and 86–8
'thing-based' vs. 'stuff-based'
ontologies and 32–4
Copp, David 91 n.
core analysis
being in pain example 95–8
canonical examples and 107–12
compatibility and 100
concept of reference in 83–8
'cycling mathematician'
example 101–2
de dicto necessity and 93–4, 102–3, 108–9
de re modality and 100–4, 109–10
'dog' example 90–1
entailment and 92–4, 100, 101–4
entity-essences and 88–9

essentialist thought experiments
and 104–7
'horse/animal' example 93–4, 100
'horse/statue' example 84–6
k-essences and 90–2
Kripke's essentialist experiments
and 103–7
Nixon example 105–7
reduction and 95–100
'wooden table' example 103–4
counterfactual uses 180
counterpart theory 63–7, 77

de dicto necessity 93–4
de re as special case of 102–3
expression in modal logic
and 108–9
reductive analysis and 60, 98–9
definite descriptions 113–14, 127, 131–2, 149, *see also* sophisticated
description (SD) theories
de re necessity
essentialism and 100–4
expression in modal logic
and 109–10
reductive analysis and 60
detached realms 60, 61–7
devices of direct reference 114–15
direct reference (DR)
theories 114–23
ambiguity in 115, 122–3
artifact case and 115–18
conflicting intuitions and 120
extensional semantics and 151–2
natural object case and 118–22
rigid designation and 127
technical names and 139
weak special sense and 122–3, 139
dispositions of users, *see* application
dispositions
DR theories, *see* direct reference
(DR) theories

eliminativism 96–7
empty names 113–14, 159, *see also*
fictional names
endurantism 9–12, 24

Index

entailment relation
 being fictional and 166–7
 de dicto necessity and 92–4, 100
 de re necessity and 100, 101–4
 essentialist thought experiments and 104–7
entity-essences, *see also* k-essences; object-essences; person-essences
 in core analysis 88–9
 necessary existence and 173
epiphenominalism 96–7
equivalence classes 28–9
error, and categories 142–3
essentialism, *see also* mereological essentialism (ME)
 expression in modal logic and 110–12
 Kripke's thought experiments and 103–7
 nontrivial *de re* necessity and 100–4
examples, *see* thought experiments
existential presuppositions 153 n.
exotic objects 24–6, 30, 36
expression/assertion strategy 167–8, 176
extensionality
 instantiation and 51, 52–3
 problems with 150–2
 Quine's notion of 48–51

fact of the matter, existence of 13–15, 34–46
Fara, Delia Graff 131 n.
Farewell, My Lovely (Chandler) 164–71
fictionalizing 168
fictional names 113, 159–77
 analogical uses of 170–1
 central facts about 159
 Chandler's 'Velma' and 164–71, 176–7
 concept of necessary existence and 171–7
 as expression of k-essences, 159–63
 fictional stance and 163–4

'Humphrey' case 171–2, 173–4
'Jack and Jill' case 160–2
literary interpretation and 170
uses outside the story 167–71
use 'within the story' 159–63, 167
fictional-person-essences 165–6, 168–9, 177
fictional stance 163–4, 167–8
first-order logic
 extensionality in 48–9
 Principle of Constitution and 56–7
 property-based view of names and 153–6
 as representation of ordinary language 150–3
 single-quantifier approach to physical reality and 84, 86–8
Fitch, Greg 90 n., 91 n., 188 n.
functional features
 categories and 143–5, 147–8
 natural kind terms and 191–2, 194–6, 197–8
fundamental objects 25–7
 Black's globes and 32
 instantaneous 26, 36
 ordinary objects and 29–31
 origins of 27–9, 31
 t-stages of 29–30
fundamental particles 24–6
fundamental point-object path 31
fundamental types 26–7, 28–9

great divide
 accommodation of, as goal 18–22
 Daffy/Venus-type cases and 121–2, 128–32
 k-essences and 91–2
 mereological essentialism and 37–40
 necessity *de re* and 101, 102–4
 physical reality and 15–22, 83–6, 120–1

haecceities 28, 32 n. 89
Heller, Mark 27
Hintikka, Jaakko 62
Hirsch, Eli 12 n.

identities of objects 22–36, *see also* fundamental objects
identity conditions 46–54
identity relation, universality of 46–7, 52–3
identity sentences 154 n.
inclusionism 97–8
instantaneous fundamental objects 26, 36
instantiation
 entailment and 92–4
 fictional names and 166, 169–70, 176–7
 first-order logic and 56–7
 'Humphrey' case and 66
 necessary existence and 173–7
 object-essences and 89
 properties and 51, 52–3, 55–7
intensional entities, *see* abstract entities
intrinsic properties
 fundamental objects 26–7
intrinsic relations 93

Jankovic, Marija 123 n.

Kaplan, David 115
k-essences, *see also* fictional-person-essences; person-essences
 in core analysis 90–2
 definite descriptions and 131–2
 fictional names and 159–63
 ordinary names and 155–7
kinds, *see also* category; great divide; natural kind terms; object fixation
 great divide and 15–22
 identity conditions and 46–53
King, Jeffrey 114, 115 n., 152 n.
Kripke, Saul 62
 causal chain view 122–3
 direct reference and 116
 essentialist thought experiments of 103–7

essentiality of material origins and 116–17
Naming and Necessity xiv, 114, 166 n., 188–96
natural kind terms and 181 n., 182 n., 186–96
Queen Elizabeth II case and 65–6
rigid designators and 126–7
semantics of modal logic and 68–72
unicorns and 166 n.
use of definite descriptions and 141
wooden table example 103–4, 117–18
world theory and 75 n.

Lewis, David xi, 79 n., *see also* possible worlds
 face value argument and xii, 41–2
 necessary properties and 171–2
 possible worlds analysis by 59–67, 70, 77
 reduction and 60, 67, 98–100
 'true in a story' and 161 n.
linguistic constructions
 extensionality and 51–3
 reduction and 99–100
literary interpretation 170
'loading-in' 115, 127, 132
logic, *see* first-order logic; modal logic
Ludwig, Kirk 174 n.

'magical ersatzism' 79 n.
Marcus, Ruth Barcan 62, 71 n.
mass quantification 5–9
Materna, Pavel 22 n.
matter, *see also* convention Q; physical object; physical reality; Q-objects
 concept of 1–2, 9
 fundamental types of 25–6
 as particle-based 24–5
 without fundamental particles 25–6

Index

meaning, *see also* category; social determination view
   contemporary theories of names and 115, 122–3, 140–1
   natural kind terms and 179–81
   property-based approach to names and 149–57
Meinong, Alexius 71
mereological essentialism (ME), 4 n., 36–40, *see also* essentialism
mind, identity theory of 95–8
misrepresentation 65–6, 168
modal exclusivity, property of 88
modality, *see* core analysis; *de dicto* necessity; *de re* necessity; possible worlds; property-based strategy
modal logic
   canonical examples and 107–12
   metaphysical analysis and 70–4
   semantics of, and world theory 67–74
   statue/clay example and 130–2
Montague, Richard 62

name-givers
   category determination and 136–7, 138–41
   fictional names and 167–8
   natural kind terms and 179–84
   ordinary names and 123, 136–7, 138–9
   technical names and 139–40
natural kind terms 179–98, *see also* k-essences
   'air' example 188, 197–8
   'gold' case 186–7, 189–97
   Kripke's discussion of 186–96
   orthodox picture of 181–3
   orthodox view with social determination and 180 n., 185–6
   problems with orthodox view of 183–6
   'tiger' example 195 n., 196
   without a posteriori necessity 179, 182–3, 196–8

'XYZ' case 181–6
natural objects, and DR theories 118–22
necessary existence, and fictional names, 171–7
necessity
   de dicto, 60, 93–4, 98–9, 102–3, 108–9
   de re, 60, 100–4, 109–10
   a posteriori, and natural kind terms 179, 182–3, 196–8

object-essences
   artifacts and 118
   de re necessity and 102–4
   entity-essences and 89
   k-essences and 90–2
object fixation
   great divide and 18–22, 86, 120–1, 129
   mereological essentialism and 37–8
   modal expression and 131–2
   necessity *de re* and 101, 102–4
objectification 6, 7, *see also* composition
objectual quantification 4–5, 6–9, *see also* convention Q
'object-variability' 34–6
ordered sets 49, 50
ordinary names 113–57, *see also* fictional names
   apparent conflict in intuitions about 120–1, 128–32
   'Bellamy Road' example 115, 124–6
   Château Margaux case 133, 135, 145
   Cloudy Mountain example 137, 138
   contemporary theories of 114–27
   'Daffy' case 115–17, 120–2, 126, 128–33, 135, 139, 140–1, 147 n.
   direct reference (DR) theories of 114–23
   'George W. Bush' example 149–57
   'The Palm' example and 143–5, 146

ordinary names (*cont.*)
  problematic cases of 141–9
  puppy naming example 136, 137
  '*Queen Mary*' example 145, 147 n.
  social determination of categories and 132–41
  sophisticated description (SD) theories of 123–7
  statue/clay example and 130–2
  'Suzie' case 143, 147
  theory of names with bearers and 149–57
  Trump examples 133–4, 135, 137, 138, 145, 146–7
  'Venus' case 118–20, 126, 128–32, 180
  'Venus/star' case 136, 138, 142
  'wooden table' example 117–18
ordinary things
  great divide and 15–22
  identity of 29–31
  persistence through time and 9–15
origin-indistinguishability 28–9

particle physics 22–3, *see also* spacetime worms
particularity, *see* identities of objects
perdurantism 133 n., 144
  convention Q and 12–15, 22
  endurantism and 9–12
person-essences 105–7, 111, 153–157
  fictional-person-essences and 165–6, 168–9
  ordinary names and 155–7
physicalist philosophy of mind 95–8
physical objects, *see also* concrete entities; convention Q; natural objects; ordinary things
  arrangement of parts and 15–22, 36–40
  conventions governing concept of 31, 34–6
  identity of 22–36
  mereological essentialism and 36–40
  persistence through time 9–15
  as posit 43–4
  quantification and 2–9
  Quine's characterization of ('Q') 1–2
physical reality, *see also* direct reference (DR) theories
  entity-essences and 88–9
  fundamental category of 86–8
  great divide and 83–6, 120–1, 128–9
  property-based strategy toward 83–8
  'stuff-based' vs. 'thing-based' ontologies of 32–4
Plantinga, Alvin 102 n.
Plato, 53, 78, *see also* Principle of Constitution; properties
plural quantification 5 n., *see also* mass quantification
point-objects 30–1, 34–5, 36
possibilism 71–2
possible worlds theory, *see also* Lewis, David
  abstract worlds and 59–60, 78–82
  actualism and 71–2, 73–4, 77–8, 125
  central tenet of 60, 67–8, 73, 74–5
  counterpart relations and 63–7, 77
  face value argument and 41–2
  fundamental weirdness in 74–6, 151 n.
  Lewis's analysis and 41–2, 59–67
  as mathematical device 68–70, 72
  modal oomph and 63–7, 77
  necessary existence and 171–2
  persuasive terminology of 60–3
  reductive analysis and 60, 67, 98–100
  semantics of modal logic and 67–74
predicate-co-expression relation 52

Principle of Constitution
  entailment and 92–4
  entity-essences and 89
  instantiation and 55–7
  speaking about things and 87
Principle of the Indiscernibility of
    Identicals 10–11, 12
proper names, *see* fictional names;
    ordinary names
properties, *see also* entailment
    relation; necessary existence;
    Principle of Constitution;
    property-based strategy
  abundance and 54–5
  assumptions about 54–7
  direct reference and 139–40
  entailment relation and 92–4, 100
  entity-essences for 89
  'face value' argument and 41–3
  fundamental types of matter as
    26
  intrinsic nature of 93, 100
  posits in Quine and 43–6
  Quine's problem of identity
    conditions and 46–54
property-based strategy 53–4, *see
    also* compatibility relation; core
    analysis; entailment relation;
    k-essences
  assumptions about properties
    and 54–7
  category and 135
  definite descriptions and 130–2
  ordinary names and 149–57
  toward physical reality 83–8
property dualism 96–7
property identity, and necessity a
    posteriori 182–3
propositions, *see also* abstract
    entities
  abstract worlds concept
    and 79–82
  DR theories and 114–15,
    151–2
  Quine and 45–6
Putnam, Hilary xiv, 181 n.
  natural kind terms and 179–80,
    181, 182 n., 184 n.

Q-objects, *see also* convention Q;
    ordinary things
  great divide and 15–22
  physical matter and 1–9
  quantification and 6–9
  spatial possibilities and 22–36
  temporal possibilities and 9–15
QPO, *see* convention Q
quantification
  modal semantics and 70–4
  objects and 2–9
  single vs. multiple view of 83–8
  use of names and 149, 153–5
'qua-objects' 121 n.
Quine, W. V.
  characterization of objects
    ('Q') 1–2, 6, 23
  identity conditions and xii–xiii,
    43, 46–54
  From a Logical Point of View
    44
  modality *de re* and 101–2
  'On What There Is' 43–4
  posits and 42–6
  'Speaking of Objects' 45–6
  Word and Object xi, 42

Ray, Greg 82 n., 174 n.
Reber, Steve 143
reductive analyses
  modality and 60, 67, 98–100
  theory of mind and 95–8
reference, concept of 83–8
representation, concept of 64–7
  intentionality and 65
  similarity and 64–5
rigid designation 126–7
rigidification strategy 124–6
Roy, Tony 73 n.
Russell, Bertrand 127, 130–1

scientific ontology 44–5
SD theories, *see* sophisticated
    description (SD) theories
set theory 49, 54, 79
Sider, Ted 3 n., 12 n., 34 n., 90 n.,
    95 n.

similarity relations 64–5, 66–7
singular objectual
    quantification 4–5
singular properties
    entity-essences and 88, 103
    k-essences and 91, 131, 155–7
    object-essences and 103
social determination view, *see also*
        fictional names; natural kind
        terms; ordinary names
    apparent conflicts with 141–9
    fictional names and 161, 165
    natural kind terms and 179–81,
        180 n., 185–6
    ordinary names and 132–49, 179
'some' as quantifier 4–5
sophisticated description (SD)
    theories 115, 123–7
spacetime, matter in 1–2, 13–14, 15,
        see also convention Q
    object location and 22–36
spacetime, regions of, *see*
    fundamental types
spacetime worms 24, 26–9, *see also*
    fundamental objects
spatiotemporally detached
    realms 60, 61–7
specificity, *see* identities of objects
Steinbrenner, George 125
stewards 135, 138–40, 146–9
storytelling 161–2, 168
'stuff-based' vs. 'thing-based'
    ontologies 32–4
synonymy 52

theoretical posits, *see also* abstract
        entities; properties
    Quine's approach to 43–6, 54
    without identity conditions 47–8
'thing-based' vs. 'stuff-based'
    ontologies 32–4
thought experiments
    'air' example 188, 197–8
    'barn' example 10–11, 12 n., 14
    'being in pain' example 95–8

'Bellamy Road' example 115,
    124–6
Black's globes and 32
Château Margaux case 133, 135,
    145
Cloudy Mountain case 137, 138
'cycling mathematician'
    example 101–2
'Daffy' case 115–17, 120–2, 126,
    128–33, 135, 139, 140–1, 147 n.
Dali museum example 17 n.
'dog' example 37–8, 90–1
'George W. Bush'
    example 149–57
'gold' case 186–7, 189–97
'horse/animal' example 75–6,
    93–4, 100
'horse/statue' example 84–6
'Humphrey' example 64–7, 171–2,
    173–4
'Jack and Jill' example 160–2
Kripke's essentialist
    experiments 103–7
Nixon example 105–7
'olive-sized object'
    example 19–20
'The Palm' example and 143–5,
    146
'puppy naming' example 136,
    137
Queen Elizabeth II case
    and 65–6
'Queen Mary' example and 145,
    147 n.
Ship of Theseus story and 16–17,
    18, 21–2
'statue/clay' example 16–17, 19, 20,
    130–2
'Suzie' case 143, 147
'tiger' example 195 n., 196
Trump examples 133–4, 135, 137,
    138, 145, 146–7
'two-piece suits' example 3–4
'Velma' case 164–71, 176–7
'Venus' case 118–20, 126, 128–32,
    180

'Venus/star' case 136, 138, 142, 184
'wooden table' example 103–4, 117–18
'XYZ' case 181–6
Tichý, Pavel 22 n.
T-paths 28–9
Trump, Donald 133–4, 135, 137, 138, 145, 146–7
truth, and world theory 60, 69–70, 73, 74, 77
truth conditions 150, 151 n.

vagueness
  constitutional differences and 91–2
  notion of necessary existence and 172, 174–5

Walton, Kendall 163 n.
water 181–6, *see also* natural kind terms
'within the story' notion 159–63, 167
world theory, *see* possible worlds theory

The manufacturer's authorised representative in the EU for product safety is Oxford University Press España S.A. of el Parque Empresarial San Fernando de Henares, Avenida de Castilla, 2 – 28830 Madrid (www.oup.es/en or product.safety@oup.com). OUP España S.A. also acts as importer into Spain of products made by the manufacturer.

www.ingramcontent.com/pod-product-compliance
Ingram Content Group UK Ltd.
Pitfield, Milton Keynes, MK11 3LW, UK
UKHW022211230426
12048UKWH00016BA/782